And I Will Trust in You Alone

A Book of Encouragement in My Journey
Against Cancer

Graham Priddy

authorHOUSE®

AuthorHouse™ UK Ltd.
500 Avebury Boulevard
Central Milton Keynes, MK9 2BE
www.authorhouse.co.uk
Phone: 08001974150

First published by AuthorHouse 3/23/2010

ISBN: 978-1-4490-7335-0 (sc)

This book is printed on acid-free paper.

Acknowledgements

Colin Bailey – initial proof read
Rolf Lamsdale – second proof read
Jan van Es – medical content proof read

Everyone who has prayed for me and my family

Dedication

I dedicate this book to my wife Ginny, who has been a tower of strength during my illness, faithfully visiting me in hospital even when I was too ill to hold a conversation for any period, and to my three boys, Chris, Richard and Daniel who have encouraged me by the depth of their Christian faith with various words, emails and texts. And finally to Lucy, who from day one has been prepared to pray for me and my family, at any time of the day or night. No matter what the problem has been, she has been petitioning Father God and has become a dear friend.

Forward

A while ago I had the privilege of meeting up with Graham. I discovered that we have a lot of things in common. We are both committed Christians. We both regularly attend Spring Harvest and we both discovered that we had been diagnosed with cancer at about the same time.

We met up in the Spring Harvest team lounge with Graham's wife Ginny and my wife Irene. We both related our cancer stories to each other and discovered yet another thing that we have in common. Although we had both experienced a really tough year, we felt that it had been even tougher for our loved ones and families.

I thought that meeting up with Graham may be a rather sad time but nothing could be further from the truth. Graham is a man full of faith and hope. He is a man who loves and trusts Jesus in the good times and still loves and trusts Jesus in the difficult times. It was such a joy to sit and talk with him. The saddest part was after a while we had to leave. Graham could not tell me when or how his cancer journey would end, but he did know that Jesus is in control of everything that is happening in his life.

Here in this book is Graham's painful story. Blunt, honest and to the point but full of personal lessons that I believe will be an encouragement to both the healthy and the less healthy. Here is a chance to walk alongside Graham on a journey that none of us humanly speaking, would choose.

Rev Ian Smale (Ishmeal)

Since 1970, Ish (Rev Ian Smale) has been travelling to many countries and ministering through word and music mostly to families and children. He has written many books and released around 40 albums. His most well known song is 'Father God I Wonder'. Today, as well as travelling to Churches he is the Missioner / Deacon at Chichester Cathedral and is also recovering from Leukaemia.

Introduction

At the outset of my cancer treatment, whilst at Spring Harvest 2008, I gave my cancer to God to use for His good, whilst wanting to be healed. Then when the news of my cancer spread, I found I quickly lost track of what I had shared with whom about my condition as people enquired how I was. Being a project manager by profession, I decided to bring this under control by writing a regular update which would also enable people to focus their prayers on the real issues at that time, rather than just generally praying for me.

I never expected that these prayer updates would become such an encouragement to so many people. So much so that on occasions people asked if they had missed one when in fact one hadn't been issued.

My son Daniel first encouraged me to write this book, which is a gathering of my regular prayer updates and which, linked together, became my diary and a replication of 'my book of encouragement' where I copied down scripture verses, songs and words that people sent me to encourage me on my journey. Much of that book contains God's promises and other wonderful gems from scripture that help me when things are tough. On the first page of that book I wrote, 'My book of encouragement as I face my cancer in the knowledge that God is in control and cares for me'. I still believe that today.

This book was originally intended to cover my year's battle against cancer, but as you will read, God had other plans for my life and so has covered a longer period which in many ways has tested my faith further, but I will leave you to draw your own conclusions as you read into the second year with my cancer having taking a different course.

As you read this book, my prayer is that you too will be encouraged and know that, despite all things, God loves you and is able to meet your needs, whatever they are, and provide the strength to carry on.

December 2007

I have finally realised after a number of months suffering with excess wind and repeatedly needing to go to the toilet that I should consult my doctor. He was very understanding and suggested that I started drinking Actimel which is a yoghurt drink which contains the bacteria probiotics which can help your body improve its immune system, therefore fighting against illnesses and diseases. I was advised if nothing had improved after a couple of weeks, I should see him again.

11 February 2008

Despite drinking the Actimel yoghurt drinks, nothing had changed; in fact things appeared to be getting worse so I decided I ought to see my doctor again. The reason I had delayed another appointment was that over the Christmas period eating habits are different and I thought this may have been part of the reason my digestive system was not working properly. However, the need to repeatedly go to the toilet was beginning to get me down and was becoming uncomfortable. Another reason for putting off this appointment was that I can't face medical situations - having previously fainted when having a simple blood test and needing to close my eyes when watching medical scenes on the TV or in films.

My doctor immediately recommended that I should go for a flexible sigmoidoscopy at the hospital where the experts could see if anything was wrong. He said that appointments are normally made within two weeks which proved to be right.

26 February 2008 – email to close family

Hi,

It's probably time to share with you that I have been suffering since before Christmas with a digestive problem and have seen the doctor a couple of times now. He has now referred me to the hospital for a flexible sigmoidoscopy next Thursday at 9.00am. This is an investigation with a camera to look at my rectum and colon. This is something I am not looking forward to especially as you're not normally sedated and I tend to faint at medical situations at the best of times.

Your prayers appreciated.

Blessings
Graham

26 February 2008 – Book of Encouragement

7   The LORD will keep you from all harm - He will watch over your life;
8   The LORD will watch over your coming and going both now and forevermore.

Psalm 121 v 7 - 8

(Email from Mum and Dad Priddy)

28 February 2008

Today I have an appointment at the Royal Berkshire Hospital for a procedure called a flexible sigmoidoscopy. The procedure is used for finding out what is causing symptoms such as changes in bowel habit or rectal pain. It is also used to check for inflammation, early signs of cancer and polyps. During the procedure, they may take biopsies (samples of tissue) for examination in a laboratory.

As the doctor has to see clearly, the bowel needs to be completely empty and when I awoke, it was necessary to use the enema I had been sent in the post. This is designed to empty your bowel within a few minutes. I did not find this easy to administer and so Ginny had to assist.

The examination only took about 10 to 15 minutes and was very uncomfortable, rather than painful, as air was pumped through the tube into the lower bowel to make it expand. This made it easier to see with the aid of a camera lens at the end of the sigmoidoscope which sent pictures from the inside of the bowel to a TV screen.

Following the examination, I was able to rest in a ward for an hour prior to being told that they had found something and I would require a further visit to the Outpatients department at a later date.

In view of the discomfort, I took the rest of the day off work and spent some time finishing off the decking I was building in the garden.

29 February 2008 – Book of Encouragement

6   Humble yourselves, therefore, under God's mighty hand, that He may lift you up in due time.

7   Cast all your anxiety on Him because He cares for you.

1 Peter 5 v 6 - 7

('Life on Lucas' Bible reading notes)

2 March 2008 – Book of Encouragement

At church today, David Partington gave me a big hug. It's good to know that he really cares and is the only person who currently knows that I have some health issues.

I was in the sound gallery doing the projection of songs, reading and sermon but found myself reflecting on 1 Peter 5 v 6 – 7. Amazing reassurance.

2 March 2008 – Book of Encouragement

This is not a spiritual song per se but, I just sense that God wants you to know He will raise you up and carry you. You can get it on: http://www.ladynwavsone.com/raisemeup.html and it plays as well as giving the words.

'You Raise Me Up' by Josh Groban

When I am down and, oh my soul, so weary;
When troubles come and my heart burdened be;

Then, I am still and wait here in the silence,
Until you come and sit awhile with me.

Chorus
You raise me up, so I can stand on mountains;
You raise me up, to walk on stormy seas;
I am strong, when I am on your shoulders;
You raise me up: To more than I can be.

(See YouTube link for full lyrics)

© The music was written by Secret Garden's Rolf Løvland and the lyrics by Brendan Graham

(Email from David Partington at Woodley Baptist Church)

6 March 2008 – Book of Encouragement

Today I go to the hospital to see the Registrar Mr Farouk and to get the result of the biopsies. However the results were inconclusive so I was advised that further tests and scans would be needed.

14 But I trust in You, O LORD;
     I say, "You are my God."
16 Let Your face shine on Your servant;
     save me in Your unfailing love.
24 Be strong and take heart,
     all you who hope in the LORD.

Psalm 31 v 14, 16 & 24

('Life on Lucas' Bible reading notes)

10 March 2008 – Book of Encouragement

I shared my health situation with the Church Leadership Team ahead of our away day on Saturday 15th. Thought this was important as we were to spend the day together and I dearly love these guys with whom I share in the leadership of Woodley Baptist Church.

11 March 2008 – Book of Encouragement

Today I go back to the hospital, this time for a CT scan. The CT (or CAT) scan will take a series of X-rays of my body from different angles. With the aid of a computer, a detailed picture of the inside of my body can be built up from the X-ray cross-sections. This will give an accurate picture of where a tumour is and how big it is. It will also show how close major body organs are to the area that needs to be treated or operated on.

A CT scanning machine is a large machine that is shaped rather like a doughnut with a couch to lie on. The couch slides backwards and forwards through the hole of the doughnut.

It's good to know that whilst I undergo various investigations and scans I'm supported in prayer.

15 March 2008 – Book of Encouragement

Today the Church Leadership went to Henley Baptist Church for an away day. Having shared the news of my cancer with them on the 10th March, it was an ideal opportunity to explain my situation in more detail at the start of this day together. After sharing, we spent a considerable period praying for God's healing and then for the focus for the day.

Felt God's peace and warmth as well as being glad that I know and trust these guys.

Thank You, God.

Footnote: following my operation I explained to these guys that we should have prayed for God's healing without operations ☺

20 March 2008 – Book of Encouragement

I go back to the hospital today, this time to see the Registrar, Mr Farouk. I awoke feeling God's peace for the day ahead, more so than my previous visit on the 6th March.

It was confirmed that I have bowel cancer and the proposed course of treatment would start on 2nd April with the proposed operation being outlined. This would be followed up by chemotherapy and then radiotherapy treatment prior to an operation to remove the tumour.

God's timing is perfect as this allows me to work at Spring Harvest in Skegness and then go with the family and church to Spring Harvest in Minehead with the operation between the two events.

Started to tell family and close friends whilst continuing to feel God's peace. David Barter, our minister at Woodley Baptist Church, came round in the evening and prayed with Ginny and me.

20 March 2008 – Email

Dear family & close friends

As you know I had an appointment with the Registrar at the hospital today and in view of your prayer support I would like to update you on my situation.

It has been confirmed that it is bowel cancer and a course of treatment has been proposed, which will start with an operation on Wednesday 2nd April when another biopsy will be taken, and the expectation is that I will need to remain in hospital for a few days. Then towards the end of April, I will commence a 12 week course of radiotherapy & chemotherapy. Following this I will require a further operation to remove the tumour.

I am expecting to get further details about the first operation on Monday 31st March when I return from Spring Harvest.

As a word of encouragement to you, I very much felt God's peace throughout the day which I'm sure is a direct result of your prayers, thank you. As I write this, I am reminded of 1 Peter 5 v 6 & 7 which says, *'Humble yourselves, therefore under God's mighty hand that He may lift you up, Cast all your anxiety on Him because He cares for you'*. And reassured by 2 verses my Dad sent me Psalm 121 v 7 & 8 *'The Lord will keep you from all harm, He will watch over your life; the Lord will watch over your coming and going both now and for evermore'.*

Blessings
Graham

20 March 2008 – Book of Encouragement

Of course Michal & I sat and prayed for you and your family as you have a rough steep road for a while. Glad to hear that you are facing it with your eyes fixed on Jesus. Hope to stand with you during this time.

(Email from Pete Evens - Woodley Baptist Church Elder)

20 March 2008 – Book of Encouragement

Remember   2   When you pass through the waters,
I will be with you;
and when you pass through the rivers,
they will not sweep over you.
When you walk through the fire,
you will not be burned;
the flames will not set you ablaze.

Reading on   3   For I am the LORD, your God,
the Holy One of Israel, your Saviour;
I give Egypt for your ransom,
Cush and Seba in your stead.
5   Do not be afraid, for I am with you;
I will bring your children from the east
and gather you from the west.

(Email from Paul and Ann Redfern at Woodley Baptist Church)

21 March 2008 – Book of Encouragement

Silently 'say'

"cast all your anxieties"	(whilst breathing in deeply)
"On Him"	(breathe out slowly)
"Because He cares"	(breathing in His presence deeply)
"for you"	(breathe out slowly)

Based on 1 Peter 5 v 7

(Email from Rev David Priddy - Brother)

22 March 2008 – Book of Encouragement

Isn't it good to know that Father God already lined up encouragement for you and the Holy Spirit got on to it? May you discover Jesus is your strength and shield and strong deliverer and power to stand in spite of pain. Psalm 91 sprang straight to mind as I read your email. It was true for Mike and me and I know it's true for you.

1   He who dwells in the shelter of the Most High
      will rest in the shadow of the Almighty.
2   I will say of the LORD, "He is my refuge and my fortress,
      my God, in whom I trust."
3   Surely He will save you from the fowler's snare
      and from the deadly pestilence.
4   He will cover you with His feathers,
      and under His wings you will find refuge;
      His faithfulness will be your shield and rampart.
5   You will not fear the terror of night,
      nor the arrow that flies by day,
6   nor the pestilence that stalks in the darkness,
      nor the plague that destroys at midday.
7   A thousand may fall at your side,
      ten thousand at your right hand,

but it will not come near you.
8   You will only observe with your eyes
    and see the punishment of the wicked.
9   If you make the Most High your dwelling—
    even the LORD, who is my refuge—
10 then no harm will befall you,
    no disaster will come near your tent.
11 For He will command His angels concerning you
    to guard you in all your ways;
12 they will lift you up in their hands,
    so that you will not strike your foot against a stone.
13 You will tread upon the lion and the cobra;
    you will trample the great lion and the serpent.
14 "Because he loves me," says the LORD, "I will rescue him;
    I will protect him, for he acknowledges my name.
15 He will call upon me, and I will answer him;
    I will be with him in trouble,
    I will deliver him and honour him.
16 With long life will I satisfy him
    and show him my salvation."

Psalm 91 v 1 - 16

(Email from Mary Hearn – Sister-in-Law)

23 March 2008 – (Easter Day) - Book of Encouragement

The Christian is not at the mercy of chance. We have placed our trust in the infinite, all powerful and all knowing God, who has taken on the final threat to us, death itself, and beaten it. He is able to steer us aright. The tomb is empty, Hallelujah.

('Life on Lucas' Bible reading notes)

24 March 2008 – Book of Encouragement

1   I lift up my eyes to the hills -
    where does my help come from?
2   My help comes from the LORD,
    the Maker of heaven and earth.

Psalm 121 v 1 - 2 plus "we live with the resurrection power of Jesus".

Read by Jeff Lucas in the Big Top at Spring Harvest in Skegness where I was serving as a volunteer in the capacity of Deputy Chief Steward.

I have been a volunteer steward at Spring Harvest since 1999 and since 2001 I have taken on more of a leadership role. Spring Harvest started life in 1979 as a one-week event for fewer than 2,000 people. Today it's a multi-week, multi-location event attended by more than 45,000 people of all ages, church backgrounds and walks of life, who come together each Easter to learn, laugh and worship. The dynamic programme helps and enables people to be stronger and closer followers of Jesus in their home, work and church.

Find out more about Spring Harvest by following the link http://www.springharvest.org/

28 March 2008 – Book of Encouragement

16 May our Lord Jesus Christ Himself and God our Father,
    who loved us and by His grace
    gave us eternal encouragement and good hope,
17 encourage your hearts and strengthen you in every good deed and word.

2 Thessalonians 2 v 16 - 17

(Day 3 at Spring Harvest by Jeff Lucas)

30 March 2008 – Book of Encouragement

31 but those who hope in the LORD
will renew their strength.
They will soar on wings like eagles;
they will run and not grow weary,
they will walk and not be faint.

Isaiah 40 v 31

(Email from Hannah Davidson – Spring Harvest Steward)

30 March 2008 – Book of Encouragement

6 being confident of this, that He who began a good work in you
will carry it on to completion
until the day of Christ Jesus.

Philippians 1 v 6

(Bill Smith - Spring Harvest Steward)

30 March 2008 – Book of Encouragement

You have always been a tower of strength and support to me and
I am so grateful. Not sure of my pastoral visiting skills but know that
I love you and thank God that He chose you to be my earthly father.
Be at peace, I love those words in your card that simply said "our God
is able".

(Text from Chris Priddy – Son)

31 March 2008

Following an active week working at Spring Harvest I returned
to work this morning in the knowledge that I needed to speak with
my team about my cancer and forthcoming treatment. I called a team

meeting and broke the news explaining that whilst cancer is a serious condition, I was totally at peace about the news and was happy to talk with people individually if required.

Shortly afterwards, I joined the managers' team meeting and again explained my news and learnt afterwards that when I left the room the ladies all cried, which I wasn't expecting. However I started to appreciate that this affects the people I know as well as my family. I prayed they would all be ok. The afternoon was filled with six other team briefings and a number of people took up the opportunity to individually talk with me afterwards.

Received several cards and loads of good wishes and prayed again that God would use my cancer for His good.

I left the office that evening in the knowledge that my job and finances were secure, having been told by senior management to forget work, focus on getting well, and return when I'm ready.

31 March 2008 – Book of Encouragement

He will watch over you while you sleep.

(Text from Lucy Tovey - Spring Harvest Chief Steward)

1 April 2008

Today at 5.00pm I go into the Royal Berkshire Hospital for my pre-operative check, following which I go to the Loddon Ward to be admitted for my operation tomorrow for a colostomy and for another biopsy. Whilst not looking forward to this I feel God's peace and Him saying "Be still and know that I am God".

A colostomy is a surgical procedure in which my colon will be cut and brought to the outside through the abdominal wall to create an artificial opening called a "stoma". My faeces will then be collected in a bag called a colostomy bag which will be attached to the opening. I have been told that this is a temporary precautionary measure to avoid my bowel becoming blocked when I start radiotherapy. The long term aim is to do a reversal at the end of my treatments.

After checking into the ward, Ginny and I went for a walk and we found the Sanctuary (church room) where we sat for a while soaking up God's peace in the quietness of that air conditioned room.

Went to bed that night thanking God for my life so far, appreciating that life from tomorrow will be different except that God is still God and I still trust Him.

1 April 2008 – Book of Encouragement

Your Saviour will never let go of you. He is by your side during the brightest of days and the darkest of nights. He IS with you always and He WILL protect you! Hope your hospital goes well.

(Text from Daniel Priddy – Son)

1 April 2008 – Book of Encouragement

PRAY

        BOLDLY
        EXPECTANTLY
        SPECIFICALLY

Your heavenly Father Loves You so don't be afraid to be Bold in Prayer

16 Let us then approach the throne of grace with confidence,
    so that we may receive mercy and find grace
    to help us in our time of need.

Hebrews 4 v 16

(Post Card from Lucy Tovey - Spring Harvest Chief Steward)

1 April 2008 – Book of Encouragement

15 And the prayer offered in faith will make the sick person well;
    the Lord will raise him up.

If he has sinned, he will be forgiven.

James 5 v 15

(Email from Neslihan Hukenek – Spring Harvest Steward)

2 April 2008 – Church Prayer Chain

Please pray for Graham and family. Graham has the first part of his treatment for bowel cancer with colostomy surgery this evening. Pray boldly that the surgery will be successful and without complications and that Graham will be able to adjust quickly to this lifestyle change. Please pray for peace for Graham, Ginny and the family.

3 April 2008 – Church Prayer Chain

Thank you for your prayers for Graham who is progressing well after yesterday's surgery. Please pray for an ongoing experience of God's peace for Graham, Ginny and family as recovery and treatment continue.

3 April 2008 – Book of Encouragement

20 Now to Him who is able to do immeasurably
more than all we ask or imagine,
according to His power that is at work within us,
21 to Him be glory in the church and in Christ
Jesus throughout all generations,
for ever and ever! Amen.

Ephesians 3 v 20 - 21

(Card from Jeff Lucas – Spring Harvest Leadership Team)

5 April 2008 – Book of Encouragement

I've read a lot of your cards from people at this time. The words that have stood out and struck me more than any other were in a card from Spring Harvest before you went into hospital. They simply said;
"Our God is Able". Amen

(Chris Priddy – Son)

6 April 2008 – Book of Encouragement

Graham, I hope you are encouraged by our reaction in seeing how great you look so soon after your operation. This is proof that the prayers of God's people and skill of the medical profession are working effectively. May God continue to bless you.

(Visit from Graeme & Marian Potts – Woodley Baptist Church Elder)

7 April 2008

First disappointment as at the last minute I heard that I wasn't going home today and needed to stay another night. I'm really glad that I have kept this book of encouragement as 'my God is able' and 'I should not be afraid as he is with me' and 'my help will be from the Lord' have really helped me get over this disappointment.

7 April 2008 – Church Prayer Chain

Graham was disappointed not to be allowed home today. Please pray that the enema given today will take effect to allow him home tomorrow.

7 April 2008 – Book of Encouragement

Message that Ann Redfern is praying for peace and assurance of God's strong arms of love holding me safe and close to Him.

20　We wait in hope for the LORD;
　　　He is our help and our shield.
21　In Him our hearts rejoice,
　　　for we trust in His holy name.
22　May your unfailing love rest upon us, O LORD,
　　　even as we put our hope in you.

Psalm 33 v 20 - 22

(Card from Ann Redfern – Woodley Baptist Church)

8 April 2008

I woke this morning in real pain as the stoma hasn't worked since the operation. My doctor changed my medication and I was also sick when dinner arrived. I forced myself to eat dinner knowing that it would do me good. God showed me during the day that despite all prayers, love and support, I would still have bad days as well as good days. Ginny sat for hours just holding my hand through the pain I was experiencing. I am so lucky to have such a wonderful wife, who has faithfully visited me every day. I have also realised the importance of having a dear friend in Lucy who has become my main prayer warrior as I'm able to text her at any time of day or night with prayer requests.

At the end of the day, I was really glad I stopped in the extra night and all of the following day; God knew all along this is what my body needed.

9 April 2008 – Book of Encouragement

Glad to see Graham home from hospital and meet with family visiting him. First stage now over and need to trust God for the coming days and anticipated treatment.

We trust you to trust the Lord for each day as it comes – some will be better than others. Prepare to be blessed at Spring Harvest – perhaps in unexpected ways. We will be there with you and for you.

Don't be slow to seek opportunities for help and support or just do chat and pray.

(Visit from Rev David Barter – Minister at Woodley Baptist Church)

9 April 2008 – Book of Encouragement

This is Mathew, who was among the Indian guys at Spring Harvest and we were praying for you. More than that, you are a living testimony for us. God already used your testimony at various places. Graham, not to embarrass you, but to say from the bottom of my heart, God loves the servant heart you have; of course you are a true steward for Christ. Thank you for your mail too which has allowed us to take a deep breath, hearing that you are fine now

"Faithful is HE, who has called you by your name"
"You aren't an accident.
You weren't mass-produced.
You aren't an assembly-line product.
You were deliberately planned,
Specifically gifted,
Lovingly positioned on this earth by the Master Craftsman."

(Email from Mathew Nathaniel – Spring Harvest Steward)

10 April 2008

Woke up all excited as after coming home from hospital yesterday after a nine day stay, today we are off to Spring Harvest at Minehead with all the family. Richard and Daniel are home and travelling with us and we are breaking the journey at Upper Stratton where Chris and Rosie will join us. It's hard to believe all that has happened since working at Spring Harvest Skegness a couple of weeks ago and that God in His perfect timing has enabled me to return to Spring Harvest with the whole family, this time as a guest. Admittedly it will be very different and I will need to rest in order to recovery fully from my operation.

We arrived at Minehead after an uncomfortable journey. When other members of our church who were also there saw me, they couldn't believe their eyes. I'm so grateful to God for making it possible and it's a real answer to prayer.

11 April 2008 – Book of Encouragement

16 Let us then approach the throne of grace with confidence,
   so that we may receive mercy and find grace to help us in our time of need.

Hebrews 4 v 16

(Taken from talk in Big Top)

13 April 2008 – Book of Encouragement

I went to the Prayer House and spent an hour and a half in the quietness and stillness of that room. I made an important decision which was 'To give my cancer to God, whilst saying that I wanted to be healed, I wanted Him to use it for His good'. Scary prayer but still prayed it.

Spent time reflecting on the following verses which were written on a board.

17 "Behold, I will create
   new heavens and a new earth.
   The former things will not be remembered,
   nor will they come to mind.
18 But be glad and rejoice forever
   in what I will create,
   for I will create Jerusalem to be a delight
   and its people a joy.
19 I will rejoice over Jerusalem
   and take delight in my people;

the sound of weeping and of crying
will be heard in it no more.

Isaiah 65 v 17 – 19

Also picked up a scroll at random from a basket following which I thought that at no stage had I questioned God as to why me as that's not important or helpful. The verse said

19 'Because I love you with an everlasting love!

Jeremiah 31 v 5

I had never spent so long in prayer and was so pleased that I had taken time out that day with God.

16 April 2008 – Prayer Newsletter 1

Hi everyone,

I have become increasingly aware of the massive prayer support that I am receiving from so many, with so many wanting updates to my situation that I have decided to prepare regular updates for everyone, instead of dealing individually which is becoming hard to manage. In this first update, if you already know some of this, then forgive me for repeating myself.

My treatment for bowel cancer commenced with an operation on Wednesday 2nd April for a colostomy and to have another biopsy taken. First biopsy taken when I had the flexible sigmoidoscopy produced inconclusive results. In all I was in hospital for eight nights. The operation has some complications but they still managed to succeed with the original plan which was clearly a better option. I have been greatly supported and encouraged by prayer support, and the medical staff were impressed with my excellent progress, despite a slight setback late Monday afternoon when I was expecting to go home. I believe this was God just telling me that on the path ahead, I will have positive and difficult days but to remain firm and keep my eyes fixed on Him.

I am now at home relaxing after having shot off to Spring Harvest in Minehead with the family the day after I was released from hospital. I used Spring Harvest as a time to relax and take it easy which was helped by hiring a wheelchair. However I did manage an odd teaching session and watched a couple which were televised from the Big Top. Chris, Rosie, Richard and Daniel all came so we had a wonderful time together. However it was a little strange as only two days prior to being admitted to hospital, I had just returned from a very active week of helping to head up a Stewarding Team at Spring Harvest in Skegness. My cancer and situation was also prayed for by name in the Big Top at Minehead yesterday which was a very humbling experience as there were approximately 3000 people there. The Head Office staff again have been so supportive.

So what's next? Firstly whilst in the Prayer House at Spring Harvest last week, I gave my cancer over to God, saying whilst I want to be totally healed, I want God to use it for His good. Medically, once I am fully recovered from the operation, which I expect to be towards the end of April, I will commence a 12 week course of radiotherapy and chemotherapy, but I expect to hear more about this when I visit the hospital on Tuesday 22nd April. Following this I will require a further operation to remove the tumour, followed by another operation to reverse the colostomy, putting me back together again.   .

I have received many words of encouragement, two dearest to my heart I will share with you as a word of encouragement for you, as I have learnt my news has totally shocked some folk, leaving some others on the verge of tears. Nonetheless I have personally very much been feeling God's peace throughout this period, which I'm sure is a direct result of the massive prayer support I have. As I write this, I am again reminded of 1 Peter 5 v 6 & 7 which says, 'Humble yourselves, therefore under God's mighty hand that He may lift you up, Cast all your anxiety on Him because He cares for you'. And reassured by two verses my dad sent me Psalm 121 v 7 & 8 'The Lord will keep you from all harm, He will watch over your life; the Lord will watch over your coming and going both now and for evermore'.

Today I have a number of appointments, telephone consultation with Doctor, Stoma Nurse early afternoon, District Nurse late afternoon, so no chance of getting bored today. I will provide a shorter update at the next key stage. If you would like to be removed from this list, do let me know.

Blessings
Graham

18 April 2008 – Book of Encouragement

4 Look to the LORD and His strength;
   seek His face always.

Psalm 105 v 4

(Email from Kevin and Libby Price – friends in Australia)

18 April 2008 – Book of Encouragement

Our Lord Jesus Christ is with you, and is interceding for you.
We have joined with Him as partners, to pray for you.
God is with you and knows what you are going through.
Never forget that HE IS WITH YOU.

(Email from Paul Ernest and the other friends from India – Spring Harvest Stewards)

19 April 2008 – Book of Encouragement

28 And we know that in all things God works
   for the good of those who love Him,
   who have been called according to His purpose.

Romans 8 v 28

2 Praise the LORD, O my soul,
   and forget not all His benefits—
3 who forgives all your sins
   and heals all your diseases,

Psalm 103 v 2 - 3

(Email from Neal & Beverley Birch – friends in Australia)

22 April 2008 – Book of Encouragement

10 Be still and know that I am God.

Psalm 46 v 10

26 I am the Lord, who heals you,

Exodus 15 v 26

1   In You o Lord, I put my Trust

Psalm 71 v 1

(Card from Paul and Ann Redfern – Woodley Baptist Church)

Today I return to the Royal Berkshire Hospital for the results of the biopsies and I believe the next stage of the treatment will be outlined to me. Psalm 105 v 4 says 'Look to the LORD and His strength; seek His face always' seems really relevant today.

22 April 2008 – Prayer Newsletter 2

Hi Everyone
First of all I would like to thank you all for your prayer support. This email is currently sent to 122 people, the church prayer chain totals105 people whilst not forgetting others in church who are actively praying for my situation and family. Words cannot express enough how grateful we are for the support we are receiving from so many.

As you will know, I had an appointment with the Registrar today and again was very reassured by God's peace both prior to and during the appointment. I even managed to deal with the internal examination this time which my Registrar explained was really important for him to carry out as the sigmoidoscopy and scans had shown the tumour to be in different locations.

During the consultation it was explained that my tumour is large and the next course of treatment was outlined as a six week course of chemotherapy combined with radiotherapy. The aim of this is to shrink the tumour which has a 60% success rate. More details of this will be explained to me when I visit the RBH Cancer Unit this Friday (25th April) at 2.30pm, along with dates for this course of treatment.

Following the chemotherapy and radiotherapy, I can expect a 10 week hiatus before an operation to remove the tumour; however this will also include moving my colostomy bag from my left to the right side of my body. As Ginny and I have always said - let's deal with this one step at a time. More about that during the summer, I guess.

I also saw my Stoma Nurse today as my stoma has become rather sore and I have been given some cream to resolve the discomfort I have. Please pray that the cream will work quickly.

Some of you will know that I am keeping 'a book of encouragement as I face my cancer in the knowledge that God is in control and cares for me'. Today the following pages in my book have encouraged me greatly.

In a card I received last night the following scripture verses typified how I was feeling and encouraged me as I read then repeatedly.

10 Be still and know that I am God.

Psalm 46 v 10

26 I am the Lord, who heals you,

Exodus 15 v 26

1   In You o Lord, I put my Trust

Psalm 71 v 1

And from a steward from Spring Harvest in Skegness and to encourage you in your prayers -

James 5 v 15 'And the prayer offered in faith will make the sick person well; the Lord will raise him up. If he has sinned, he will be forgiven'.

Unfortunately my appointment on Friday clashes with when I had hoped to pop into work to see colleagues. Please pray that another opportunity will arise shortly as currently I am unable to drive and need to fit in with Ginny's shifts.

Blessings
Graham

(Mailing list 122)

22 April 2008 – Book of Encouragement

22 Because of the LORD'S great love we are not consumed,
    for His compassions never fail.
23 They are new every morning;
    great is Your faithfulness.

Lamentations 3 v 22 – 23

(Email from Rev David Priddy – Brother)

23 April 2008 – Book of Encouragement

24 "The LORD bless you
    and keep you;
25 the LORD make His face shine upon you
    and be gracious to you;
26 the LORD turn His face toward you
    and give you peace."

Numbers 6 v 24 – 26

(Email from Jane Mitchell – Spring Harvest Steward)

23 April 2008 – Book of Encouragement

Don't Worry – The Lord is with you.

9 Who does great things and unsearchable,
Marvellous things without number

Job 5 v 9

(Email from Veera Swany Dhas – Spring Harvest Steward)

23 April 2008 – Book of Encouragement

19 And my God will meet all your needs according to His glorious riches in Christ Jesus.

Philippians 4 v 19

(Email from Les Godden – Spring Harvest Steward)

23 April 2008 – Book of Encouragement

Just went to my Bible and found these words and want to pass them on to you:
You are a valuable person
You are a special person
You are a unique person
You are a beautiful person
You are unrepeatable
You are mysterious
You are a beautiful human person
No one will ever exist like you
You are so special and valuable that Jesus died for you
His love is completely and totally 100% for you
His love is unconditional

As you keep trusting God through this very difficult time, He's with you 100%. We are standing with you and Ginny with that same trust and commit to praying for you every day. You are both two very special people and God is holding you in His mighty hand.

(Email from Andrew and Dot Butler – Woodley Baptist Church)

25 April 2008 – Prayer Newsletter 3

Hi Everyone

The visit to the Berkshire Cancer Unit this afternoon outlined the next stage of my treatment and also confirmed that cancer hadn't been found elsewhere within my body. However my tumour is 7cm long.

It is planned - but still to be confirmed - to start my chemotherapy on Tuesday 6th May, but this is subject to an appointment/operation to install a Hickman catheter (a central line) under local anaesthetic into my chest. The Fluorouracil, or 5FU as it is known, (chemotherapy drug) will be drip fed into this line 24 hours a day for six weeks. This will require weekly visits to the Cancer Unit for top-ups plus an additional visit the day before for blood tests. After a few weeks, this treatment will be combined with radiotherapy.

Nothing seems straightforward, as five days before the operation I have to complete a course of Staphylococcus Aureus (MRSA) Decolonisation Therapy which is basically a special body wash and nasal ointment.

Today was extremely helpful with loads of leaflets to read outlining the detail of the treatment plus the possible side effects which I will not expand on as the drug affects everyone differently. It has been suggested that I do not return to work until the chemotherapy is underway and my body's reaction is assessed.

This next stage in my overall treatment is extremely important and Ginny and I appreciate that some of the days ahead will be extremely difficult. However we enter it in the knowledge that *'Our God shall supply all our needs according to His riches in glory by Christ Jesus'* (Philippians 4 v 19) and I am reminded looking in my book of encouragement that "Our God is able". Thanks Chris. Finally from our dear friends Kevin and Libby in Australia who wrote we will continue to *'Look to the Lord and His strength, seeking His face always'* (Psalm 105 v 4)

Prayer requests are simple:-
    ❖ That the treatment will be 100% effective.
    ❖ The side effects will be minimal and bearable.

Blessings
Graham

25 April 2008 – Book of Encouragement

19 And my God will meet all your needs according to His glorious riches in Christ Jesus.
Philippians 4 v 19

7   But blessed is the man, who trusts in the LORD,
     whose confidence is in Him.
8   He will be like a tree planted by the water
     that sends out its roots by the stream.
     It does not fear when heat comes;
     its leaves are always green.
     It has no worries in a year of drought
     and never fails to bear fruit."

Jeremiah 17 v 7 – 8

(Email from Kevin Lowen – Woodley Baptist Church)

25 April 2008

Today I had a consultation at the Royal Berkshire Hospital Cancer Unit to outline the forthcoming treatment. I was advised that the tumour was 7cm long but there were no signs of cancer anywhere else.

The next phase of my treatment will be to install a Hickman Catheter (a central line) into my chest for the chemotherapy drug

(Fluorouracil or 5FU for short) to be pumped into me 24 hours a day, 7 days a week for about seven weeks. Five days prior to the Hickman line being installed, I will need to shower using an anti- MRSA wash. Once the chemotherapy course is underway, I will then start a course of radiotherapy which will be 5 days a week for 5 weeks.

The aim of this treatment is to downsize the tumour before the main treatment starts. In my case the combination of chemotherapy and radiotherapy is to be given before surgery, to reduce the size of the rectal tumour and therefore make it more operable. It is also used so that less radical surgery is required to remove it.

Today's visit was really helpful as what lies ahead was explained, with all possible side effects being discussed and I was given a considerable number of leaflets to read concerning what we had been told.

Ginny and I came away from the appointment realising how important the next phase of treatment is and that there are some difficult days ahead, but that 'Our God will supply all our needs according to His riches in glory by Christ Jesus'. (Philippians 4 v 19) and that Our God is able,

What is a Hickman Line?

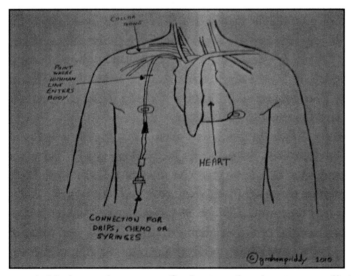

A Hickman line is a soft plastic tube that is tunnelled beneath the skin, with the tip sited in a large vein close to the heart. The catheter can be used to give fluids and drugs and for taking blood samples, so

avoiding the need for repeated needle pricks during treatment. Each lumen will have a clamp in place, which is used to close the catheter when it is not in use.

How is the Hickman Line inserted?

The Hickman line will be inserted using a local or general anaesthetic. During the procedure two incisions (cuts) will be made in my chest. The catheter will be inserted through an incision near the collar bone and then the end will be tunnelled under the skin to come out on my chest wall. Afterwards I will have two stitches, usually the top stitch will be removed around 7-10 days post insertion and the bottom stitch is kept in place for 2-3 weeks. The catheter is then flushed once a week when the next week's blood sample is required.

How does chemotherapy work?

Chemotherapy involves the administration of cytotoxic drugs (this literally means drugs which are toxic to cells) either intravenously or as a tablet, with the aim of killing any cancerous cells in your body. Although normal cells in your body will also be affected by chemotherapy, they have a great ability to repair themselves, whereas the cancerous cells are dividing more rapidly and are more vulnerable to the effects of the chemotherapy. There are many different types of chemotherapy drugs as different drugs have been found to be effective at treating different types of cancer. The drug or combination of drugs depends upon the type of cancer and the stage of the disease.

Chemotherapy is usually given in cycles – this means a series of treatments at set intervals, for example every three weeks, for a set period. The reason for this is so that the normal cells in your body have an opportunity to repair themselves after each treatment, and a larger proportion of cancerous cells can be targeted over a longer period of time. Spacing out the cycles of chemotherapy in this way aims to reduce the extent of its side effects, whilst increasing the effectiveness at actually treating the cancer. However for my treatment, it will be given 24 hours a day, 7 days a week.

How does radiotherapy work?

Radiotherapy is given to directly target the specific area in your body, usually the cancerous tumour itself, or an area where the tumour has been. Radiotherapy involves using radiation to damage the cancerous cells, to try and cause them to die. As with chemotherapy, radiotherapy is usually given in small doses (fractions) over a pre-determined length of time. In my case this was 25 treatments, being every Monday to Friday for five weeks. This is so that more cancerous cells can be targeted over the duration of the treatment and (as with chemotherapy) normal cells have the chance to repair themselves between treatments.

26 April 2008 – Book of Encouragement

14 Is any one of you sick? He should call the
elders of the church to pray over him
and anoint him with oil in the name of the Lord.

15 the prayer offered in faith will make the sick person well;
the Lord will raise him up. If he has
sinned, he will be forgiven.

16 Therefore confess your sins to each other and pray
for each other so that you may be healed.
The prayer of a righteous man is powerful and effective

James 5 v 14 – 16

8 We do not want you to be uninformed,
brothers, about the hardships
we suffered in the province of Asia.
We were under great pressure, far beyond our ability
to endure, so that we despaired even of life.

9 Indeed, in our hearts we felt the sentence of death.
But this happened that we might not rely on
ourselves but on God, who raises the dead.

10 He has delivered us from such a deadly
peril, and He will deliver us.

On Him we have set our hope that He
will continue to deliver us,

11 as you help us by your prayers. Then many
will give thanks on our behalf for the
gracious favour granted us in answer to the prayers of many.

1 Corinthians 1 v 8 - 11

(Email from Roger and Pat Snelling – friends in Sherborne)

26 April 2008 – Book of Encouragement

7   My peace I leave with you; my peace I give you.
I do not give to you as the world gives.
Do not let your hearts be troubled and do not be afraid.

John 14 v 27

(Email from Thomas Mitchell – Spring Harvest Steward)

26 April 2008 – Book of Encouragement

1   Those who trust in the LORD are like Mount Zion,
which cannot be shaken but endures forever.
2   As the mountains surround Jerusalem,
so the LORD surrounds His people
both now and forevermore.

Psalm 125 v 1 – 2

(Email from David Stillman – Woodley Baptist Church Elder)

27 April 2008 – Book of Encouragement

1   You O Lord are my God. I will acclaim
You and praise Your name,

for You have done marvellous things,
fulfilling Your age old purpose,
dependable and certain.

Isaiah 25 v 1

2 He said: "The LORD is my rock, my
    fortress and my deliverer;
3a my God is my rock, in whom I take refuge,
50 For this, O Lord I will praise You before all people,
    And I will sing praises to Your name.

2 Samuel 22 v 2, 3a & 50

14 I Praise You Lord, for I am astonishingly
    and awesomely made,
    Your works are truly wonderful;
    My Soul knows it full well.

Psalm 139 v 14

(Book by Nick Fawcell – How to Pray)

29 April 2008 – Book of Encouragement

14 This is the confidence we have in approaching God:
    that if we ask anything according to His will, He hears us.

Reading further onto the next verse

15 And if we know that He hears us
    whatever we ask - we know that we
    have what we asked of Him.
1 John 5 v 14 – 15

(Email from Linda Morgan – Work Colleague)

1 May 2008 – Book of Encouragement

Hi - a group of people from my church would like to meet you and your family and pray with you. So if it is possible for you and your family to come to my church on a Sunday and stay for lunch (a Turkish meal) with me and my British family I live with. My church is in Coalville – Leicestershire.

(Email from Neslihan Hukenek – Spring Harvest Steward)

2 May 2008 – Book of Encouragement

1   "God is our protection and our strength.
    He always helps in times of trouble.
2   So we will not be afraid even if the earth shakes
    or the mountains fall into the sea"

Psalm 46 v 1 – 2

(Email from Clare Whittaker – Nottingham)

6 May 2008 – Prayer Newsletter 4

Hi Everyone

Trust you all had a wonderful Bank Holiday weekend. The main excitement for Ginny and me was that the person we employed to finish off our garden which I was no longer able to do - namely lay a new lawn and paving under my gazebo - completed the work. As I started work on this garden project last October by laying a large decking area, you will appreciate our excitement that it's all done.

Today (Tuesday 6th May) effectively starts the next phase of my treatment with a trip to the hospital for another blood test. This will now become a weekly trip, the day before my visits to the Berkshire Cancer Unit.

I have also been challenged by (James 5 v 14) *'Is anyone among you sick? Let him call for the elders of the church, and let them pray over him, anointing him with oil in the name of the Lord.'*- thanks Roger and Pat. This is being arranged for this evening

Tomorrow (Wednesday 7th May) I have an appointment at 9.00am for a small operation to install a Hickman catheter (a central line) into my chest. Following this, I am taken to the x-ray department to check that the catheter was correctly installed.

Then at some point during the day, they will connect me up to a small portable pump (the size of a small music player) into which the chemotherapy drug will be drip fed 24 hours a day. This will then require weekly visits to the Cancer Unit for top ups. I am expecting to be at the hospital for most of the day.

As I explained in my last newsletter, this next stage in my overall treatment is extremely important and Ginny and I appreciate that some of the days ahead will be extremely difficult. However we enter it in the knowledge that *'Our God shall supply all our needs according to His riches in glory by Christ Jesus'* (Philippians 4:19).

Prayer requests are simple:-
 ❖ That the treatment will be 100% effective
 ❖ The side effects will be minimal and bearable
 ❖ The central line will be inserted without problems
 ❖ Sleeping each night will not be a problem

Finally, thank you for committing to pray for Ginny and me, and my boys Chris, Richard and Daniel. Maybe I shouldn't be surprised by the support I am receiving, but I am amazed by the practical help with lifts, offers of weekend retreats (when I'm well enough to travel) and others who have involved their own church to pray for us.

I leave you with another verse from my book of encouragement, *'This is the confidence we have in approaching God; if we ask anything according to His will He hears us'.* (1 John 5 v 14) - thanks Linda.

Blessings
Graham

(mailing list = 233)

6 May 2008

Being challenged by the verse sent to me by Roger & Pat Snelling on 26 April: James 5 v 14 which says *'Is any one of you sick? He should call the elders of the church to pray over him and anoint him with oil in the name of the Lord'*, I met with David Barter (Minister) and Elders for prayer and anointing with oil.

This was a very special time and I was really glad of the timing as my next phase of treatment, which I'm not looking forward to, will begin tomorrow. Another verse, *'And my God will meet all your needs according to His glorious riches in Christ Jesus'* from Philippians 4 v 19 came to mind.

6 May 2008 – Church Prayer Chain

Please pray that Graham, Ginny and family will continue to experience God's amazing peace as Graham has a small operation tomorrow at about 9am to insert a catheter into his chest so that during the day he can start his chemotherapy treatment.

7 May 2008

Today my Hickman line goes in and my course of chemotherapy begins. It's a lovely sunny day, however I'm not looking forward to going to hospital but I'm trusting God and claiming His promises, especially the one from Psalm 121 v 7-8 *7 'The LORD will keep you from all harm - He will watch over your life; 8 The LORD will watch over your coming and going both now and forevermore'.*

Just after getting up the hospital rang and explained that my appointment had been cancelled due to illness. Pleased that I was able to have breakfast now, but disappointed that I had planned for this appointment up to this point especially with meeting David and the Elders the night before.

I was given a new appointment for 12 May 2008 and told to continue to use the anti-MRSA shower wash for another five days prior to the procedure.

7 May 2008 – Prayer Newsletter 4.1

Dear All,

Following a series of phone calls this morning, all my hospital appointments today have been cancelled until Monday 12th May at 2.00pm This is due to the lady who installs the Hickman catheter being off sick.

Thank you for your prayers, love and concern.

Blessings
Graham

7 May 2008 – Book of Encouragement

17 How precious it is Lord,
To realise that You are thinking about me constantly!

18 I can't even count how many times a day
Your thoughts turn towards me.
And when I awake in the morning,
You are still thinking of me.

Psalm 139 v 17 - 18

(Email from Mark and Linda Hallett – Woodley Baptist Church)

7 May 2008 – Book of Encouragement

Our God is a great big God
And He holds us in His hands
Praise the Lord

(Email from Paul and Ann Redfern – Woodley Baptist Church)

7 May 2008 – Book of Encouragement

31 What, then, shall we say in response to this?
   If God is for us, who can be against us?
38 For I am convinced that neither death nor life,
   neither angels nor demons, neither the present nor the future,
   nor any powers,
39 neither height nor depth, nor anything else in all creation,
   will be able to separate us from the love of God that is in Christ
Jesus our Lord.

Romans 8 v 31, 38-29

(Email from Jonathan and Alison Frater – Spring Harvest
Steward)

8 May 2008 – Book of Encouragement

Day really dragging and want to be at work as I have been off now
since 2nd April and missing the challenge and the people I work with.
However when the post arrived, I opened one letter sent to me by my
dear friend Lucy and to my surprise it contained an A3 sheet of paper
and simply said, Galatians 6 v 11.

"See what large letters I use as I write to you with my own hand!"

This really made me laugh and cheered me up; remember thinking she's a real nut case but I really appreciate her love and support.

8 May 2008 – Book of Encouragement

We have been praying for you at every staff gathering and are committed to doing this. We want you to know that you are a part of our community and family. Stay close to God.

(Email from Wendy Beech-Ward – Head of Marketing, Spring Harvest Steward)

10 May 2008 – Book of Encouragement

17 ....but to put their hope in God, who richly provides us with everything for our enjoyment.

1 Timothy 6 v 17

(Email from Rev David Priddy – Brother)

10 May 2008 – Book of Encouragement

Keep being 'Sure and Steadfast' with your hope in God.

(Email from Robin Gunston – Friend in New Zealand)

12 May 2008 – Prayer Newsletter 5

Hi Everyone

Thank you for your prayers today and I can confirm that the Hickman line was installed perfectly on the first attempt. As I wasn't looking forward to this operation, my eyes were drawn in my book of encouragement to Isaiah 43 v 5 which reads *"Do not be afraid, for I am with you"* and also to Psalm 56 v 3 *"when I am afraid, I put my trust in you"*. We really can draw such strength from God's word when we are in need.

So I'm at home now, just a little sore which is only to be expected and with the line successfully installed, I'm all plumbed up to my chemotherapy and the proud owner of a small blue bag which will now follow me around 24 hours a day for the next 7 weeks. Next chemotherapy appointment is next Tuesday 20th May (Ginny's Birthday) so that they can refill my bag.

Off to the hospital again tomorrow afternoon for x-rays so that they can draw a target on my body for when the radiotherapy begins in a few weeks.

The rest of the week will be recovering from today's operation and understanding how my body reacts to the chemotherapy and what side effects I will need to deal with. However, I placed my order for the tiredness one, but I do appreciate it doesn't work like that.

To finish, I have to leave you with one scripture verse I received in the post from a dear friend which really made me laugh out loud. It was written on A3 paper and as the photo below shows, simply said Galatians 6:11 which read *"See what large letters I use as I write to you with my own hand!"* - thanks Lucy

Thanks again
Blessings
Graham

17 May 2008 – Prayer Newsletter 6

Hi Everyone

A number of people have asked me how things are going since I started my chemotherapy treatment on Monday and now seems an appropriate time to provide an update.

Be encouraged as I strongly believe that your prayers have sustained me as currently I haven't experienced any real side effects, just the odd tingling (pins and needles) in the arms the last couple of evenings, nothing more. I am reminded of Psalm 28 v 7 which reads *'The Lord is my strength and shield; I trust Him with my whole heart and so am sustained, My heart sings for joy within me as I give thanks to Him'*. This verse also links to the song I was listening to this week on my iPod.

> As the deer pants for the water,
> So my soul longs after You.
> You alone are my heart's desire,
> And I long to worship You.
> Chorus
> You alone are my strength, my shield,
> To You alone may my spirit yield -
> You alone are my heart's desire,
> And I long to worship You.

See YouTube link for full lyrics at http://www.youtube.com/watch?v=YY0t6_V1OqQ

© Martin Nystom 1983 Restoration Music Ltd/Sovereign Music UK

As I write this I am smiling. I mentioned in my last update that as far as side effects go, I placed my order for the tiredness one. My problem is that I tend to wake up between 5.00am and 5.30am and then need to get up as lying in bed becomes uncomfortable. This means that I tend to nod off in the evening although Ginny would say - what's new about that?

Reflecting back on the week, the most painful part of my treatment to date was when the nurse changed the dressing and removed the old one over my Hickman line yesterday. She said it's a bit like waxing (not that I have any experience of waxing my legs ☺). One of the highlights of the week was on Thursday when a number of work colleagues visited me and we enjoyed lunch together. I am so fortunate that my work, boss and colleagues remain extremely supportive of my situation.

The week ahead is a series of appointments,

Monday morning
  ❖ District Nurse visits for my weekly blood test
Tuesday morning
  ❖ Berkshire Cancer Unit for my weekly chemotherapy top up and health check
Thursday morning
  ❖ Berkshire Cancer Unit to see the Radiotherapist to discuss my treatment plan
Current prayer requests:-
  ❖ That the treatment will be 100% effective
  ❖ The side effects will be minimal and bearable
  ❖ Sleeping pattern will improve

Thanks again
Blessings
Graham

20 May 2008

It's Ginny's birthday and I am so fortunate that God has blessed me with a wonderful wife and friend. Unfortunately my chemotherapy drug got lost at the hospital today so after my weekly check up I wasted four hours just sitting around. However I have learnt to take a book, drink and my iPod these days to help pass the time. Came away totally washed out but needed to get to the supermarket to buy tonight's dinner which I had promised Ginny I would cook.

I was also reminded by two friends to just 'Be still and know that I am God' and that 'God created rest' and that this is a season where my main focus is dealing with my health and recovery.

25 May 2008 – Book of Encouragement

7   The LORD is my strength and my shield;
     I trust in Him, with all my heart and so I am sustained.
     My heart sings for joy within me
     as I give thanks to Him in song.

Psalm 28 v 7

(Book by Nick Fawcell – How To Pray)

24 May 2008 – Prayer Newsletter 7

Hi Everyone

Well it's been a frustrating week in some respects having spent hours sitting in hospital waiting rooms due to my chemotherapy drug being mislaid on Tuesday and then unsigned forms at the radiotherapy department on Thursday. Then I needed to arrange for the District Nurse to make an extra visit to change my dressing.

Being someone who dislikes poor time management I'm learning to pack my iPod, a book, a drink and just go with the flow. It's also slightly frustrating having to take various medical supplies and contact details with me at all times. Having a shower almost requires a full project plan. However, I'm reminded of Al Murray's phrase in his book, 'Publicans Guide To British Pubs' - 'mustn't grumble'. ☺.

Following Tuesday's appointment I was totally exhausted until late Wednesday evening. However, I have been reminded that God created rest and also of Psalm 40 v 10 *'Be still and know that I am God'*. In my reflections on my health treatment so far and how the chemotherapy pump works, I'm drawn to Psalm 139 v 14 which states *'I praise You Lord, for I am astonishingly and awesomely made; Your works are wonderful, my soul knows it full well'*.

Currently I still haven't experienced any real side effects despite a strong chemotherapy drug dose, just the odd tingling, (pins and needles) in the arms and fingers, nothing more, and when I popped into the office on Thursday to meet colleagues, I was repeatedly told how well I looked (must be all that relaxing in the garden ☺). My work was also having a charity day raising money for Beating Bowel Cancer, (www.beatingbowelcancer.org) which was encouraging. My white blood cells are reducing in number so I am becoming more likely to catch infections and I have been warned that if I get a high temperature of 38o to contact the doctor or hospital straight away.

The week ahead is a series of appointments:

Tuesday
- ❖ 8.30am Visit to Hospital for blood test, then Berkshire Cancer Unit for my weekly chemotherapy top up and health check
- ❖ Afternoon District Nurse for dressing change

Thursday
- ❖ 11.30am Berkshire Cancer Unit to commence my radiotherapy

Friday
- ❖ 11.30am Berkshire Cancer Unit for radiotherapy

To explain the radiotherapy, I will now be receiving this treatment every day for five weeks, excluding weekends and like the chemotherapy it has a number of side effects which I won't bore you with. However I'm not looking forward to this treatment as I found the simulation session this week extremely uncomfortable and disliked being left all alone in the machine for ten minutes while the radiotherapist moved into the control room. I need to find a way of coping with the 25 sessions (that's 4 hours 20 mins).

Current prayer requests:-
- ❖ That the treatment will be 100% effective
- ❖ The side effects will be minimal and bearable
- ❖ I will not catch any infections
- ❖ I will find a way of coping with the radiotherapy

Thanks again
Blessings
Graham

29 May 2008 – Book of Encouragement

7   Where can I go from Your Spirit?
     Where can I flee from Your presence?
8   If I go up to the heavens, You are there;
     if I make my bed in the depths, You are there.
9   If I rise on the wings of the dawn,
     if I settle on the far side of the sea,
10 even there Your hand will guide me,

Psalm 139 v 7 – 10

(Email from Roger and Pat Snelling – Friends in Sherborne)

31 May 2008 – Prayer Newsletter 8

Hi Everyone

This week saw the commencement of my Radiotherapy treatment and, as I previously explained, this was something I wasn't looking forward to as I found the simulation session last week extremely uncomfortable and disliked being left all alone in the machine for 10 minutes or so while the radiotherapist moved into the control room.

On Thursday morning (first treatment session), my Bible reading highlighted 1 Chronicles 16 v 34 *'Give thanks to the LORD, for He is good; His love endures forever'*. Later that morning I picked up my Bible again and it fell open at Psalm 118 v 1, (I will leave you to look this one up). Wondered if God was having a laugh with me, but decided I had better give thanks for the radiotherapy session ahead ☺.

So how did it go? It was fine and less frightening than the previous scan and simulation sessions. This was helped by the radiotherapist putting on the latest Mandate CD I took with me. Thanks for the suggestion Anne.

In view of expected side effects, I have been given special cream to use twice a day, been told to only use baby soap, and I have been given an ample supply of mouthwash, anti-sickness pills and tablets to treat diarrhoea, as well as having to drink five pints a day.

On Tuesday, my chemotherapy dose was reduced in view of the forthcoming radiotherapy and I again spent just over four hours at the hospital that day. Whilst I was informed that my white blood cells are continuing to reduce leaving me more likely to catch infections, my kidneys and liver are fine. I find it amazing that they can tell so much from a blood test but am encouraged that all is going well. However I have noticed that I am becoming more tried than before, getting up later and I even went back to bed after my radiotherapy session on Friday afternoon for a snooze.

The doctor has signed me off work now until 25th June which has disappointed me as I miss both the challenging and exciting environment in which I work plus my colleagues who have to cope without me but remain extremely supportive. However when you look at my appointment schedule for the week, realistically this would only be possible on three afternoons.

So as I reflect on the week, I strongly believe that your prayers have continued to sustain me and Psalm 63 v 5 - 7 sums it up nicely. *'I am contented deep within, like someone who has enjoyed a sumptuous meal. When I awake at night, reflecting during the hours of darkness over all You have done, my mouth worships You, songs of joy on my lips, for You have helped me, encircling me in the shadow of Your wings'.*

I have also taken encouragement this week from the following song called 'Who is there like you,' especially the last verse.

Last verse

And I'm trusting in Your word,
Trusting in Your cross,
Trusting in Your blood
And all Your faithfulness,
For Your power at work in me
Is changing me.

For full lyrics see YouTube link http://www.youtube.com/watch?v=n7e1ECgn7H8

© Paul Oakley, 1995 Thannkyou Music

The week ahead my appointment schedule is:
Monday
- ❖ morning District Nurse for blood tests and dressing change
- ❖ 15:20pm Radiotherapy

Tuesday
- ❖ 10:20am Chemotherapy and weekly health check at Cancer Unit
- ❖ 16:00pm Radiotherapy

Wednesday
- ❖ 11:40am Radiotherapy

Thursday
- ❖ 11:20am Radiotherapy

Friday
- ❖ 11:20am Radiotherapy

Health being ok, Ginny and I have accepted an invitation of a weekend break at Roger and Pat Snelling's in Sherborne, Dorset for some additional rest and relaxation (6th -8th June).

Current prayer requests:-
- ❖ That the treatment will be 100% effective
- ❖ The side effects will be minimal and bearable
- ❖ I will not catch any infections
- ❖ That I will not experience any skin irritation/soreness during the radiotherapy
- ❖ I will be well enough for our weekend break.

My prayer for you is that God encourages you as you continue to support me with your prayers.

Blessings
Graham

P.S. A few have asked after my brother David - he is now home from hospital recovering from his operation and doing ok.
(mailing list 239)

1 June 2008

I travelled to Coldharbour Lane Baptist Church in Hayes today as it was Chris's farewell Sunday service after spending three years there training with OASIS to become a Youth Minister. It was a privilege to be there and see how he had impacted the lives of the youngest in that church during his three year degree placement with OASIS. During the service we sang this song written by Sally-Ann Fatkin, one of the members there who gave me verbal permission to share this.

Keep me close to You, Lord
Keep me close to You
Welcomed into Your loving embrace
Marvelling still at such generous grace
Keep me close to You

Resting here with You, Lord
Resting here with You
Gently held in such powerful arms
Moved by love, I'll stay close to Your heart
Resting here with You.

© Sally-Ann Fatkin 2008

1 June 2008 – Book of Encouragement

Circle me Lord
Keep calm within
Keep storms without

Circle me Lord
Keep hope within
Despair without

Circle me Lord
Keep Strength within
Keep weakness out

Circle me Lord
Keep peace within
Keep turmoil out

(Email from Christine Joyce – Friend)

2 June 2008 – Book of Encouragement

9   "Have I not commanded you?
    Be strong and courageous.
    Do not be terrified; do not be discouraged,
    for the LORD your God will be with you wherever you go."

Joshua 1 v 9

(Internet – www.lc-words.com)

4 June 2008 – Book of Encouragement

As I was praying through prayer requests, particularly as you go into the hospital, I had very strong impression of two warrior angels standing either side of you - they were both ready for action outwards and fully protecting you - ministering to your needs - moving in obedience to Jesus.

(Email from Mary Hearn – Sister-in-Law)

6 June 2008 – Prayer Newsletter 9

Hi Everyone

Wow! I have just finished day 7 of my radiotherapy course, only 18 to go (who's counting? – me ☺ as I still don't enjoy lying face down on that hard bench). Today the machine froze twice so treatment took even longer as they had to get the engineer to reboot the computer controlling the machine. However I have drawn much encouragement from an email from my sister-in-law Mary who shared with me that whilst praying for me, she had a 'very strong impression of two warrior angels standing either side of me – both were ready for action outwards and fully protecting me, ministering to my needs and moving in obedience to Jesus'. I also drew encouragement this week from Joshua 1 v 9 *'Be strong and courageous. Do not be afraid or discouraged, for I am the Lord your God, and I will be there to help you wherever you go'*

Medically everything seems to be going well, with the doctors being pleased that I am still looking so good (didn't I always? ☺ – no need to answer that one) and my blood tests are as they would expect. However, I do now get tired after each radiotherapy treatment with Tuesdays being the worst when I seem to spend most of the day at the hospital. This week I even managed to watch a whole movie on my iPod whilst waiting to have my chemotherapy bottle changed after first seeing the doctor. Also on Tuesday I had a small procedure done to remove the clip that kept my Hickman line in place as the line has now fully graphed to my skin.

Altogether I have spent just over 12 hours at the hospital this week and am beginning to get to know some of the other patients who I see regularly.

The song that has encouraged me this week has been:-

Faithful One, so unchanging.
Ageless One, You're my rock of peace.
Lord of all, I depend on You,
I call out to You
Again and again,
I call out to You
Again and again.

For full lyrics see YouTube link http://www.youtube.com/
watch?v=Uxviwvjyg1w

© Brian Doerksen, 1989 Mercy/Vineyard

The week ahead my appointment schedule is:

Monday
- ❖ 9:10am Radiotherapy
- ❖ 11.30am District Nurse for blood tests and dressing change

Tuesday
- ❖ 10:00am Chemotherapy and weekly health check at Berkshire Cancer Unit
- ❖ 13:00pm Radiotherapy

Wednesday
- ❖ 17:00pm Radiotherapy

Thursday
- ❖ 14:10pm Radiotherapy

Friday
- ❖ 12:00pm Radiotherapy

Prayers have clearly been answered this week, especially as I have been well enough to take up Roger and Pat's invitation to enjoy a welcome weekend break in Sherborne for some additional rest and relaxation

Current prayer requests remain:-

- ❖ That the treatment will be 100% effective
- ❖ The side effects will be minimal and bearable
- ❖ I will not catch any infections
- ❖ That I will not experience any skin irritation/soreness during the radiotherapy

Blessings
Graham
(Mailing list 240)

11 June 2008 – Book of Encouragement

1   My soul finds rest in God alone;
    My salvation comes from Him.
2   He alone is my rock and my salvation;
    He is my fortress, I will never be shaken.
5   Find rest, O my soul, in God alone;
    my hope comes from Him.
6   He alone is my rock and my salvation;
    He is my fortress, I will not be shaken.

Psalm 62 1-2 & 5-6

(Email from Lucy Tovey – Spring Harvest Chief Steward)

11 June 2008 – Book of Encouragement

1   I will praise You, O LORD, with all my heart;
    before the "gods" I will sing Your praise.
2   I will bow down toward Your holy temple
    and will praise Your name
    for Your love and Your faithfulness,
    for You have exalted above all things
    Your name and Your word.
3   When I called, You answered me;
    You made me bold and stout-hearted.

8   The LORD will fulfil His purpose for me;
     Your love, O LORD, endures forever -
     do not abandon the works of Your hands.

Psalm 138v 1-3 & 8

(Email from Rev David Priddy – Brother)

14 June 2008 – Prayer Newsletter 10

Hi Everyone

Since I started writing these updates I have become aware that some people actually look forward to receiving them each week where my original intention was to just write them at each key stage of treatment. I am also very much aware from feedback that some people are encouraged by them. ☺. That said this week's is a little harder to write as, from the outset, I have been totally open about treatments and feelings. Anyhow, here we go.

This week I have found the daily trip to the hospital for my radiotherapy tedious to say the least especially with appointments being at various times in the day and delays always occurring. Wednesday's was again delayed by an hour, and I wasn't seen until 6.00pm leaving me too worn out to attend my discipleship group that evening. I have also become more aware that I am not able to commit myself to 'normal activities' or play a full part in my church leadership role.

Medically the doctors are still pleased, however the success of the chemotherapy and radiotherapy will not be known until six to eight weeks after the course finishes when I have a series of scans and consultations. However my skin is now beginning to suffer around the target area from the daily radiotherapy dose and, having just finished day 12, I still have another 13 sessions to go. At times this can be extremely uncomfortable and I chose to see the Doctor today who advised that this was normal at this stage. I reminded myself that I mustn't grumble as I'm still able to sit down (most of the time).

Ginny and I had a wonderful break last weekend with Roger and Pat and we were looked after extremely well and returned home well rested and refreshed. This weekend my son Richard has come home for four or five days between finishing university and starting work. This is something I have been looking forward to all week.

The song that has encouraged me this week was one that was written and sang at Coldharbour Lane Baptist Church during Chris's farewell Sunday service on 1st June 2008.

Keep me close to You, Lord
Keep me close to You
Welcomed into Your loving embrace
Marvelling still at such generous grace
Keep me close to You

Resting here with You, Lord
Resting here with You
Gently held in such powerful arms
Moved by love, I'll stay close to Your heart
Resting here with You.

© Sally-Ann Fatkin 2008

The week ahead my appointment schedule is:

Monday
- ❖ 9:30am Radiotherapy
- ❖ 11.00am District Nurse for blood tests and dressing change

Tuesday
- ❖ 10:40am weekly health check at Berkshire Cancer Unit
- ❖ 11.20am Radiotherapy
- ❖ 1.00pm Chemotherapy

Wednesday
- ❖ 8.50am Radiotherapy
- ❖ Morning check up with Stoma Nurse

Thursday
- ❖ 9.10am Radiotherapy

Friday
- ❖ 9.20am Radiotherapy

Current prayer requests remain:-

- ❖ That the treatment will be 100% effective with the tumour shrinking
- ❖ That the skin irritation and soreness will not worsen during the radiotherapy
- ❖ I will cope with the early morning radiotherapy appointments and my stoma
- ❖ I will not catch any infections

This week I will leave you with my favourite portion of scripture from Ephesians 1 v 2-14 which always encourages me. However it would be great to receive a reply with your favourite portion of scripture.

2 Grace and peace to you from God our Father and the Lord Jesus Christ. 3 Praise be to the God and Father of our Lord Jesus Christ, who has blessed us in the heavenly realms with every spiritual blessing in Christ. 4 For He chose us in Him before the creation of the world to be holy and blameless in His sight. In love 5 He predestined us to be adopted as His sons through Jesus Christ, in accordance with His pleasure and will – 6 to the praise of His glorious grace, which He has freely given us in the One He loves. 7 In Him we have redemption through His blood, the forgiveness of sins, in accordance with the riches of God's grace 8 that He lavished on us with all wisdom and understanding. 9 And He made known to us the mystery of His will according to His good pleasure, which He purposed in Christ, 10 to be put into effect when the times will have reached their fulfilment - to bring all things in heaven and on earth together under one head, even Christ. 11 In Him we were also chosen, having been predestined according to the plan of Him who works out everything in conformity with the purpose of His will, 12 in order that we, who were the first to hope in Christ, might be for the praise of His glory. 13 And you also were included in Christ when you heard the word of truth, the gospel of your salvation. Having believed, you were marked in Him with a seal, the promised Holy Spirit, 14 who is a

deposit guaranteeing our inheritance until the redemption of those who are God's possession - to the praise of His glory.

Ephesians 1 v 2-14

Blessings
Graham

P.S. Please continue to pray for my brother David, as the hospital advised him on Tuesday that the healing process is taking longer than expected, and for a full recovery for my sister-in-law Janet who is now home following her breast cancer operation this week.

15 June 2008 – Book of Encouragement

"Never give in—never, never, never, never, in nothing great or small, large or petty, never give in except to convictions of honour and good sense. Never yield to force; never yield to the apparently overwhelming might of the enemy."

Sir Winston Churchill, Speech, 1941, (1874 - 1965)

38 For I am convinced that neither death nor life,
    neither angels nor demons,
    neither the present nor the future, nor any powers,
39 neither height nor depth, nor anything else in all creation,
    will be able to separate us from the love of
    God that is in Christ Jesus our Lord.

Romans 8 v 38-39

(Email from John Hearn – Nephew)

21 June 2008 – Prayer Newsletter 11

Hi Everyone
This week has been the worst so far. Firstly on Monday the District Nurse was unable to draw blood from my Hickman line meaning I

needed an extra visit to the hospital ward to take the blood samples that were needed prior to my chemotherapy appointment on Tuesday.

By Wednesday evening I was in a lot of discomfort and, after mentioning this to the Radiotherapist on Thursday morning and in consultation with my Colorectal Specialist nurse, I was informed that I have acquired a large (bed) sore just above the treatment area. I found this slightly disappointing as when I saw the Doctor last Friday he advised me there was nothing wrong despite the discomfort I was already in. I'm now awaiting delivery of a special cushion as sitting down isn't the best experience just now. During the week I also suffered from a number of mouth ulcers (one of the possible side effects) which are now under control by using the special mouthwash I was given. I have also needed to sleep most afternoons and stayed in bed Saturday morning as I felt generally unwell. Whilst in bed this morning God reminded me of the following song words;

Be still and know that I am God (repeat 3 times)
I am the Lord, that healeth thee (repeat 3 times)
In Thee, O Lord, do I put my trust (repeat 3 times)

Traditional Author unknown

During this difficult week, I was reminded of Isaiah 40 v 31 *'But those that hope in the Lord will renew their strength,'* -Thanks Hannah and Hebrews 4 v 16 *'Let us then approach the throne of grace with confidence, so that we may receive mercy and find grace to help us in our time of need.'*

Last week I particularly asked for prayer that I would cope with the early morning radiotherapy appointments and my stoma. Thank you, as my body clock adjusted itself on those three early mornings resulting in everything being fine.

Monday was significant as this was the half way point of my radiotherapy treatment, I have now had 17 sessions, just 8 to go and I'm already thinking about how to celebrate the completion of this treatment phase.

Friday was great as my whole team visited me over lunchtime. Not only was it good to see them, but this ongoing contact with work colleagues means so much to me as does the supportive environment in which I work. They brought with them a large Helium filled balloon with a sunshine face on, so I now have an ongoing reminder of the visit. Thanks team. ☺

The song that has encouraged me most this week is Amazing Grace; in fact I listened to it repeatedly on Friday and drew strength from verse 2 and 3.

> Amazing grace, how sweet the sound
> That saved a wretch like me,
> I once was lost, but now am found,
> Was blind, but now I see.
>
> 'Twas grace that taught my heart to fear
> And grace my fears relieved;
> How precious did that grace appear
> The hour I first believed.
>
> Through many dangers, toils and snares
> I have already come,
> 'Twas grace that brought me safe thus far,
> And grace will lead me home.
>
> When we've been there a thousand years,
> Bright shining as the sun;
> We've no less days to sing God's praise,
> Than when we first begun.

John Newton (1725 - 1807)

The week ahead my appointment schedule is:

Monday
  ❖ 9:30am District Nurse for blood tests and dressing change
  ❖ 11.20am Radiotherapy
Tuesday
  ❖ 10:30am Weekly health check and chemotherapy top

up
- ❖ 12:30pm Radiotherapy

Wednesday
- ❖ 9:10am Radiotherapy

Thursday
- ❖ 16:20pm Radiotherapy

Friday
- ❖ 9:00am Radiotherapy

Current prayer requests remain:-
- ❖ That the treatment will be 100% effective with the tumour shrinking
- ❖ That the skin irritation and soreness will quickly heal
- ❖ I will cope with the early morning radiotherapy appointments and my stoma
- ❖ I will not catch any infections

Thanks to those who forwarded your favourite portion of scripture, they were interesting to see and so encouraging to read.

Blessings
Graham

22 June 2008 – Book of Encouragement

8   He has showed you, O man, what is good.
And what does the LORD require of you?
To act justly and to love mercy
and to walk humbly with your God.

Micah 6 v 8

(Email from Beverley Bailey – Woodley Baptist Church)

22 June 2008 – Book of Encouragement

Whatever your situation, whatever you are facing, you don't have to face it alone. Speak to God in prayer.

16 "Don't urge me to leave you or to turn back from you.
   Where you go I will go, and where you stay I will stay.
   Your people will be my people and your God my God.
17 Where you die I will die, and there I will be buried.
   May the LORD deal with me, be it ever so severely,
   If anything but death separates you and me

Ruth 1 v16–17

(Email from John Miller – Friend)
Note: The above verse was our Wedding Text.

22 June 2008

Oh how good God has been to me as I end this week knowing that I only have three more radiotherapy treatments to go and this phase of my treatment will be finished.

I praise God as I haven't really had any side effects, just a few mouth ulcers, a bit tired on occasions and in the last few days, an unexplained bed sore or minor piles.

I am 100% convinced that Prayer has sustained me during this period.

27 June 2008 – Prayer Newsletter 12

Hi Everyone

One of the reasons for these prayer letters is that it enables everyone to pray meaningfully for my current needs as Psalm 17 v 6 says *'I call on You, O God, for You will answer me; give ear to me and hear my prayer'*. Well prayers have certainly been answered this week as I haven't experienced any further mouth ulcers, I have been less tired, the discomfort I was experiencing last week has reduced and I have spent less time in hospital waiting rooms.

I have also felt more positive within myself as on Tuesday I was advised that I no longer needed to attend the Tuesday morning clinics as I am now on my last chemotherapy bottle. (As the radiotherapists insisted my bottle had to have a name, I called it Noah. This was due to me having it for 40 days and 40 nights and like Noah's ark, it's similar to a box and it involves fluid! ☺ - OK so I have a strange sense of humour). Also, with only three more radiotherapy sessions left, I have agreed with my Doctors that I should be able to return to work on 14th July. However, this is dependent on any side effects which I have been told may peak within a week and a half of the treatment ending.

Unfortunately as this week ends, the Doctor has informed me today that I am suffering from first degree piles (a possible side effect) which explains my current discomfort, but looking on the bright side, it could be a lot worse.

During the week I came across the following prayer which is so relevant that I thought I would share it with you.

> I do not know what life may hold,
> if good or ill I'll see
> what twist and turns may yet unfold,
> what trials yet might be.
>
> I cannot say if light will shine
> or darkness fall once more,
> what destiny might still be mine,
> what future lies in store.
>
> But even if the way is tough
> and storms begin to blow,
> the gales prove strong, the water rough,
> one thing, Lord, still I know:
>
> That You'll be there, supporting me,
> a faithful, loving guide –
> a constant help who will not fail
> to strengthen and provide.
>
> I have no need to ask for more
> nor any cause to fear;

whatever life may hold for me
I know that You'll be near.

The week ahead my appointment schedule is:
Monday
- ❖ 9:30am District Nurse to flush my Hickman line and change dressings
- ❖ 17:10pm Radiotherapy
Tuesday
- ❖ 9:30am Radiotherapy
- ❖ 10:00am Farewell to Noah - chemotherapy bottle disconnected ☺
Wednesday
- ❖ 9:10am Radiotherapy – last treatment ☺
- ❖ 9:30am Minor operation to remove Hickman line ☺

It is worth explaining that when the radiotherapy sessions end, the radiotherapy continues to work on the tumour for another 6-7 weeks. After this it will be possible to have a series of scans to establish that the tumour has shrunk prior to the next phase of treatment.

Current prayer requests remain:-
- ❖ That the tumour will continue to shrink
- ❖ I will cope with the operation and that the Hickman line is removed easily
- ❖ The piles will quickly heal
- ❖ That I can recharge my batteries prior to returning to work.

Blessings
Graham

4 July 2008 – Prayer Newsletter 13

Hi Everyone
This has been an emotional week as I finished both chemotherapy and radiotherapy; I am now hospital appointment free until the end of

August. However I have to admit that by Monday I had had enough of travelling to the hospital every day for radiotherapy despite having two more sessions to go. So when I had my last session on Wednesday followed by my Hickman line being removed, I celebrated with a WRVS cuppa and a slice of ginger cake (I highly recommend the ginger cake if you are ever at the Berkshire Cancer Unit).

Despite finishing the radiotherapy sessions, as I explained last week, the radiotherapy continues to work on the tumour for approximately six weeks; however I was warned again on Wednesday that any side effects will peak in the next week. Currently the only side effect I have is that my backside is extremely sore, so much so it sometimes keeps me awake at nights.

So with the second phase of my treatment drawing to a close and reflecting back, it's been a long journey since 28th February when I had the flexible sigmoidoscopy appointment, following which a dear friend sent me the following song which seems relevant. At the time it made me cry and if you wish to listen to it, click on the following link http://www.ladynwavsone.com/raisemeup.html

When I am down and, oh my soul, so weary;
When troubles come and my heart burdened be;
Then, I am still and wait here in the silence,
Until you come and sit awhile with me.

Chorus
You raise me up, so I can stand on mountains;
You raise me up, to walk on stormy seas;
I am strong, when I am on your shoulders;
You raise me up: To more than I can be.

© The music was written by Secret Garden's Rolf Løvland and the lyrics by Brendan Graham

Whilst not written by a Christian, the words of the chorus can imply God's strong support in difficult times. As you will know from my previous updates, I have very clearly felt God holding my hand every step of the way and have so much to be thankful for. Today so many scriptures and songs come to mind. However, I will quote from:

Psalm 86 v 12 *"I thank You Lord God, with my whole heart, and will give glory to Your name for ever, for great is the constancy of Your love to me"*

and

Act 2 v 26 *"I brim over with happiness, my words overflow with joy. Human though I am, I rest assured in hope",*

Appreciating I am now about a third of the way through my overall treatment plan.

Current prayer requests remain:-

- ❖ That radiotherapy will continue to work and shrink the tumour
- ❖ All soreness will quickly heal including my piles
- ❖ A good night's sleep
- ❖ That I can recharge my batteries enough prior to returning to work on 14th July.

Blessings
Graham

(Mailing list 242)

11 July 2008 – Prayer Newsletter 14

Hi Everyone

On Thursday my daily Bible reading was Romans 5 v1-5 *'1 Therefore, since we have been justified through faith, we have peace with God through our Lord Jesus Christ, 2 through whom we have gained access by faith into this grace in which we now stand. And we rejoice in the hope of the glory of God. 3 Not only so, but we also rejoice in our sufferings, because we know that suffering produces perseverance; 4 perseverance, character; and character, hope. 5 And hope does not disappoint us, because God has poured out His love into our hearts by the Holy Spirit, whom He has given us'.*

This reading highlights that we should be glad as we have the opportunity for an even deeper, more mature faith as we steer through tough times with God's help. The reading also reflects various aspects of my week which, whilst being hospital free, hasn't been without suffering. Sunday evening to Tuesday lunchtime I had an extremely bad headache, spending periods resting in bed. Added to this, the soreness, discomfort and piles didn't improve until late Thursday, and Wednesday evening my stoma started playing up. This has meant that I am still not sleeping well. However, whilst suffering, opportunity has existed to enjoy the peace that only God provides and to be thankful for God's amazing grace, looking forward to pain free days, appreciating that this experience has been positively changing my character.

The week has also had its highs; I celebrated being hospital free by cooking a barbeque for 28 last Sunday lunchtime for my discipleship group, made complete with a fly past by the red arrows display team. Ginny and I celebrated our 26th Wedding Anniversary. I also enjoyed my first 'normal' shower in 10 weeks which didn't require a full project plan or special manoeuvres (funny how simple things become significant events) and this Saturday I am going on a prayer retreat near Oxford.

One of my favourite songs at church is taken from Psalm 23. This Psalm has a special place in my heart as Mike (my Brother-in-law) read it to close family members in the knowledge that he was dying of bile duct cancer. I think you will agree that this famous piece of scripture provides such strength, comfort and reassurance to those who love and trust our great God.

Verse 1
The Lord's my Shepherd; I'll not want.
He makes me lie in pastures green.
He leads me by the still, still waters,
His goodness restores my soul.

Chorus
And I will trust in You alone,
And I will trust in You alone,
For Your endless mercy follows me,
Your goodness will lead me home.

For full lyrics see YouTube link http://www.youtube.com/watch?v=HzQHMtxp-RM&feature=related

On Monday, after 15 weeks off I will be returning to work, starting with mornings (9.30am to 1.00pm) and working on a number of short term initiatives. In view of further treatment, I have agreed with my boss that this will add greater value than returning back to my previous role for a short while.

To conclude, I will leave you with the following verses from Lamentations 3 v 22 – 24, *22 'The steadfast love of the LORD never ceases, His mercies never come to an end; 23 they are new every morning; great is Your faithfulness. 24 "The LORD is my portion," says my soul, "therefore I will hope in Him."*

Current prayer requests are:-
- ❖ I will cope with returning to work
- ❖ The tumour will continue to shrink
- ❖ All soreness will completely go this week
- ❖ For a good night's sleep, which would be nice

Blessings
Graham

11 July 2008 – Book of Encouragement

23 The steadfast love of the LORD never ceases,
    His mercies never come to an end
23 They are new every morning;
    great is Your faithfulness.
24 I say to myself, "The LORD is my portion;
    therefore I will hope in Him."
Lamentations 3 v 22-24

(Email from Graeme Potts – Woodley Baptist Church Elder)

12 July 2008 – Book of Encouragement

> In Him
> We Live
> We Move
> And have our being

(Prayer Retreat – Richard Pickles – Woodley Baptist Church)

12 July 2008 – Book of Encouragement

Reflections at Prayer Retreat

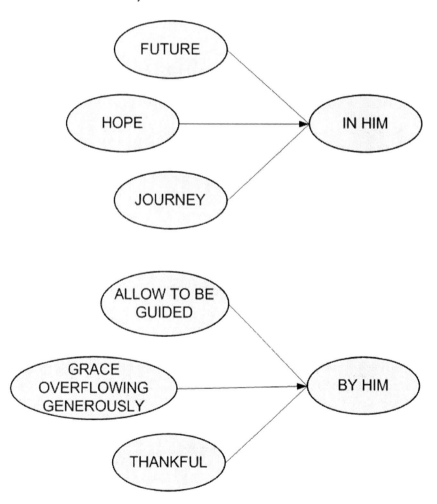

Great Wife
Amazing Family
Great prayer support
Spring Harvest
Good employment

12 July 2008 – Book of Encouragement

27 Peace I leave with you; my peace I give you.
I do not give to you as the world gives.
Do not let your hearts be troubled and do not be afraid.

John 14 v 27

(In person - Karen Taylor – Woodley Baptist Church)

19 July 2008 – Prayer Newsletter 15

Hi Everyone

Well, it's Friday and I have survived the experience of returning to work. I have to admit it was a little strange walking into the office after so long, but good to get back for a number of reasons, in particular it's the first bit of normality since my operation 16 weeks ago. Everyone was so pleased to see me back and most of Monday was spent talking to people, and on Friday I recommenced what has become a Friday afternoon tradition of walking round the department with the biscuits, which I suspect was another reason they were so pleased to see me back. In all honesty, I don't feel I have done that much and I have needed a nap most afternoons, but it's been great to get back even if it is only 9.30am to 1.00pm.

Next Wednesday, Ginny and I go on holiday to Dublin for three days (http://www.clontarfcastle.ie/) and then travel to Wexford for a week (http://www.warrenfarmireland.com/coach_house.htm) returning 2nd August. Therefore I have decided that this will be my last prayer letter until the next phase of treatment begins towards the end of August. I then expect to have a couple of scans prior to an appointment with my Consultant on 1st September to confirm the details of my next operation.

Yesterday I was given a gift from my son Chris. It was a marble tablet with the words 'Prayer makes all things possible'. How true this is and I thank you all for your faithfulness in praying for me and my family these past months. Some of you will recall that in my first prayer letter I explained that whilst in the prayer house at Spring Harvest I gave my cancer over to God, saying whilst I wanted to be totally healed, I wanted God to use it for His good. I was encouraged again today when it was mentioned that many people have been greatly encouraged by these weekly prayer letters. With all this in mind, please join me with a thankful heart by singing to yourself, or even out loud, the Doxology.

Praise God, from whom all blessings flow,
Praise Him, all creatures here below;
Praise Him above, ye heavenly host,
Praise Father, Son, and Holy Ghost.

In recent weeks, three people have given me the following scripture John 14 v 27 where Jesus said to His followers, *"Peace I leave with you, my peace I give you, I do not give as the world gives. Do not let your hearts be troubled and do not be afraid."* And everyone said Amen.

Current prayer requests are:-
- ❖ The tumour will continue to shrink
- ❖ Patience as I await dates for the various scans and the outcome
- ❖ An enjoyable holiday (with sunshine!)

Finally can I ask you to pray for my brother David, his wife Eileen and daughter Kathryn? It is a very long and emotional story but on Tuesday they are all going to St George's Hospital at 3.00pm to see a kidney transplant surgeon together with their friend Ron who has been undergoing tests as a live donor. Other potential donors for Kathryn have 'fallen by the wayside' before this penultimate step so we are asking for your prayers for Ron and Kathryn that day. If all is well they may get a date for a transplant, or a target at least. Please pray for God's will, not theirs, the doctors or anyone else's to be done.

Have an excellent summer; next update will be at the end of August.

Blessings
Graham

30 August 2008 – Prayer Newsletter 16

Hi Everyone

In my last prayer letter on 19 July I finished by wishing you all an excellent summer and that my next update would be at the end of August. So here we are at the end of August, hopefully all a little browner, all relaxed after our holidays ☺ and as a few of you have said to me how much you have missed my weekly updates, smile as the wait is over.

Our summer holiday to Southern Ireland was wonderful despite the limited sunshine, however it did bring home to me that I did not have the stamina to walk as far as I would have liked and made me realise that my body has had to cope with so much since treatment commenced 2 April 2008. The highlight of the holiday was going to the theatre in Dublin to see Riverdance. Then over the Bank Holiday weekend, we travelled to Erpingham in Norfolk and spent a fantastic break with Tony and Jacky Peacock who used to attend our Church.

I have been coping OK, having returned to work part time (9.30am to 1.00pm) and it's been great to have some normality back into my life and once again being able to add some value to a company that has supported me so well during my illness.

So, after an eight week break, I received a phone call from the hospital last Wednesday lunchtime asking me to attend that afternoon for an MRI scan and also a CT scan. Both scans meant a lengthy visit of 2.5 hours but I'm well prepared these days with iPod and book so time soon passes.

The scans were in preparation for next week's hospital appointments when I hope to find out that the tumour has shrunk and the details of my next operation.

My appointments are:

Monday
- ❖ 10:10am Clinic appointment at Berkshire Cancer Unit

Thursday
- ❖ 15:20pm Appointment with my Consultant

Current prayer requests are:-
- ❖ That I will cope with the news about the success (or not) of the previous treatments
- ❖ The date of my operation will fit in with the need to get Daniel to Aberystwyth University on 20th September.

Other exciting news is that next Saturday at 3.00pm, my eldest son Chris will be ordained as a Baptist Minister Youth Specialist, with him taking up his first ministry the following Sunday at Upper Stratton Baptist Church near Swindon.

In my last update, I mentioned my brother David, his wife Eileen and daughter Kathryn. The good news is that Kathryn is scheduled for a kidney transplant on 1st October.

Finally I will leave you with a song I discovered last weekend entitled 'There is a Hope' by Mark Edwards and Stuart Townsend,

There is a hope burns within my heart
That gives me strength for every passing day
A glimpse of glory now revealed in meagre part

Yet drives all doubts away
I stand in Christ with sins forgiven
And Christ in me the hope of heaven
My highest calling and my deepest joy
To make His will my home

For full lyrics see CD There Is A Hope - Live Worship from Ireland by Stuart Townend.

© Stuart Townsend/Mark Edwards, 2007 Thankyou Music

Blessings
Graham

1 September 2008

It's almost two months since I finished radiotherapy and going back to work is proving OK and it's good to have some normality back into my life after months of hospital appointments. I've been going into the office at 9.30am and leaving at 1.00pm, working on special tasks as opposed to managing my team. After work I have an afternoon nap and then commence decorating the two small bedrooms.

Ginny and I enjoyed a wonderful holiday in Southern Ireland and the rest of the summer was good.

I went back to the hospital this morning and I was advised that chemotherapy and radiotherapy treatment has had a significant impact on reducing the tumour – Praise God as this will make the forthcoming operation to remove the tumour easier.

1 September 2008 – Prayer Newsletter 17

Hi Everyone
Psalm 106 v 1 says *"Give thanks to the LORD, for He is good; His love endures forever"*. I quote this as encouragement to you all who have faithfully prayed for me as the hospital confirmed this morning that the chemotherapy and radiotherapy has had a significant impact on reducing the tumour.

At Thursday's appointment I should receive details of my next operation. Thank you for your support and enjoy rejoicing as indeed I am.

Blessings
Graham

2 September 2008 – Book of Encouragement

Rejoice, the Lord is King!
Your Lord and King adore;
Mortals, give thanks and sing,
And triumph evermore:
Lift up your heart, lift up your voice;
Rejoice! Again I say; Rejoice.

(Email from Norman Priddy – Father)

4 September 2008

Today I saw my Registrar, Mr Farouk, who advised me that my operation to remove the tumour would be on Monday 13th October 2008. During the operation, they would close off my colostomy and do an ileostomy.

Mr Farouk tried to do an internal examination to establish how low down the tumour was but this had to be aborted due to the pain it was causing me. He will now have to wait until I'm on the operating table to establish the position of the tumour.

Praise God as things are moving forward.

5 September 2008 – Prayer Newsletter 18

Hi Everyone
Following on from the good news at Monday's appointment that the chemotherapy and radiotherapy has had a significant impact on reducing the tumour, I saw the Registrar on Thursday afternoon to discuss details of my next operation. To my surprise he wanted to carry

out another internal investigation to establish exactly where the tumour is. This can only be described as extremely unpleasant and very painful (still suffering this morning) and was aborted after two attempts. This means that they will now have to wait until the operation to check this out.

My operation will be on Monday 13th October being admitted the afternoon before. This operation will involve removing the tumour and also closing off the previous colostomy and doing an ileostomy. (i.e. moving my stoma from the left side of my body to the right). I understand this operation is more major than my previous operation and I should expect to be in hospital for at least a week, which means I will be celebrating my 51st birthday in hospital and sadly will miss Chris's graduation day.

However, once again your prayers have been answered as this date means that Ginny and I will be able to move Daniel to Aberystwyth University on 20th September, stay overnight and return the next day. Well, a different sort of weekend break ☺. Previous thoughts of a late holiday in the sun after all my treatments this year are now not likely to materialise.

My father explained to me earlier this week that he was reminded of an old hymn by Charles Wesley (1707-1788)

Rejoice, the Lord is King!
Your Lord and King adore;
Mortals, give thanks and sing,
And triumph evermore:
Lift up your heart, lift up your voice;
Rejoice! Again I say; Rejoice.

Yes, I/we have so much to rejoice about and I am still very much rejoicing following Monday's news with the following two scriptures coming to mind; *'You are worthy, O Lord our God, to receive glory, honour and power, for all things were made by You, their creation and existence is down to You'.* Revelation 4:11 and *'Be joyful always; pray continually; give thanks in all circumstances, for this is God's will for you in Christ Jesus'.* 1 Thessalonians 5 v 16 to 18

You have guessed by now that I am still very much in a joyful and thankful mood, and before finishing I would like to share with you this old prayer of St John Chrysostom (c347-407) which reminds us of the sovereignty of God.

Blessed are You, Lord God of our fathers,
To be praised and exalted above all for ever –
Blessed be Your glories and holy name,
Yours, Lord, is the greatness and the power,
The glory, victory and majesty,
For everything in heaven and earth is Your
Yours is the kingdom,
and You, Lord are exalted as the head over all,
we will sing a new song to You Lord.

Current prayer requests are:-
❖ I remain fit and well so that the operation can proceed as planned
❖ That I can lose the weight gained by not being so active prior to my operation

Blessings
Graham

(Mailing list 243)

19 September 2008 – Prayer Newsletter 19

Hi Everyone

Well, it's been two weeks since my last update and with two weeks before my next hospital appointment this seems a sensible time to hit the keyboard again.

Seems a lot has happened from a family viewpoint. I attended Chris's (eldest son's) ordination service on 6th October, a personal goal I had set myself many months ago. As a bonus I was also able to attend his induction service last Sunday when Rev Chris Priddy became the Upper Stratton Baptist Church Baptist Minister Youth Specialist. A very proud moment. With my brother David, there are now two Rev Priddy's in the family.

This weekend, Ginny and I are hiring a van and moving Daniel (youngest son) to Aberystwyth University, staying nearby overnight and returning the next day.

Despite all this excitement I am finding the wait until my operation a little difficult, becoming increasingly aware that the operation is more major than before and, in some way, looking forward to my 'Fit for Surgery Assessment' on 6th October when I can establish exactly what to expect and timescales for recovery.

The following song has become very special to me, as it was the final song when I was working at Spring Harvest Skegness just days before my first operation and was also the final song at Chris's induction service last weekend. The words provide such reassurance that God is bigger than my cancer. The first verse and chorus are below but you can listen to the full version at http://www.youtube.com/watch?v=-08YZF87OBQ.

Everyone needs compassion
Love that's never failing
Let mercy fall on me
Everyone needs forgiveness
The kindness of a Saviour
The hope of nations

Chorus
Saviour, He can move the mountains
My God is mighty to save
He is mighty to save
Forever, Author of salvation
He rose and conquered the grave
Jesus conquered the grave

© Ben Fielding & Reuben Morgan, 2006 Reuben Morgan and Ben Fielding/ Hillsong Publishing/kingswaysongs.com

Having been invited to work again at Spring Harvest next year, this time week 3 at Minehead, I pray that this will mark the end of a long journey with real encouragement to those who stood and prayed with me at the commencement of my treatment.

My father has provided me with great encouragement during my illness, and I have quoted him several times in these updates. Can I ask you please to pray for him as on Monday 22nd September he is due to have day surgery for some recently discovered skin cancer on the top of his head?

Current prayer requests are:-
- ❖ God's amazing peace will surround me, and calm me in this period of waiting
- ❖ I remain fit and well so that the operation can proceed as planned
- ❖ The weight loss will continue prior to my operation ☺
- ❖ My father's surgery and recovery will go well

Blessings
Graham

22 September 2008 – Book of Encouragement

28 "Come to me, all you who are weary and burdened,
   and I will give you rest.
29 Take my yoke upon you and learn from me,
   for I am gentle and humble in heart,
   and you will find rest for your souls.
30 For my yoke is easy and my burden is light."

Matthew 11 v 28-30

27 Peace I leave with you; my peace I give you.
   I do not give to you as the world gives.
   Do not let your hearts be troubled and do not be afraid.

John 14 v 27

1   God is our refuge and strength,
    an ever-present help in trouble.
2   Therefore we will not fear, though the earth give way
    and the mountains fall into the heart of the sea,
3   though its waters roar and foam
    and the mountains quake with their surging.
4   There is a river whose streams make glad the city of God,
    the holy place where the Most High dwells.
5   God is within her, she will not fall;
    God will help her at break of day.
6   Nations are in uproar, kingdoms fall;
    He lifts His voice, the earth melts.
7   The LORD Almighty is with us;
    the God of Jacob is our fortress.
8   Come and see the works of the LORD,
    the desolations He has brought on the earth.
9   He makes wars cease to the ends of the earth;
    He breaks the bow and shatters the spear,
    He burns the shields with fire.
10 "Be still, and know that I am God;
    I will be exalted among the nations,
    I will be exalted in the earth."
11 The LORD Almighty is with us;
    the God of Jacob is our fortress.
    Selah

Psalm 46 v 1-11

(Email from Mary Hearn – Sister-in–Law)

5 September 2008 – Book of Encouragement

20 Now to Him who is able to do immeasurably
more than all we ask or imagine,
according to His power that is at work within us,

Ephesians 3:20

(Email from Audrey and Byron Goulding – Woodley Baptist Church)

11 October 2008 – Prayer Newsletter 20

Hi Everyone

As I write this, I'm very much aware of the tremendous love and prayer support I have as I approach the third phase of my treatment, an operation which I'm calling the 3 in 1. The operation is to:-

1. Remove the tumour by removing the piece of bowel that contains the cancer and then joining up the two open ends.
2. Closing off my colostomy (previous operation)
3. Carrying out an ileostomy

Steps 2 and 3 effectively move my stoma from the left side of my body to the right. The current plan is to be able to reverse the ileostomy after a few months, i.e. putting my digestive system back together again so that everything works as before. This is highly desired from my viewpoint.

My operation will be on Monday 13th October and I will be checking into Loddon Ward at 6.00pm the day before. I have been told I can expect to be in hospital for just over a week which means I will be celebrating my 51st birthday in hospital and sadly will miss Chris's graduation.

I have to admit to being a little apprehensive about this major surgery and will once again draw strength from Psalm 121 v 7 & 8 *'The Lord will keep you from all harm, He will watch over your life; the*

Lord will watch over your coming and going both now and for evermore'. I found myself repeating this verse over and over on the day of my last operation.

On the inside cover of my book of encouragement which I started on 26th March 2008 at the outset of my treatment, I wrote 'My book of encouragement as I face my cancer in the knowledge that God is in control and cares for me'. As I approach my next operation, I have been reflecting on an entry emailed to me more recently by Graeme Potts from Lamentations 3 v 22-24 which reminds me that; *'The steadfast love of the LORD never ceases, His mercies never come to an end; they are new every morning; great is Your faithfulness. "The LORD is my portion," says my soul, "therefore I will hope in Him."*

Two other pages have also jumped out at this time, the first a song I heard at Coldharbour Lane Baptist Church, written by a church member, Sally Anne Fatkin. The words are tremendous:

> Keep me close to You, Lord
> Keep me close to You
> Welcome into Your loving embrace
> Marvelling still at Your generous grace
> Keep me close to You
>
> Resting here with You, Lord
> Resting here with You
> Gently held in such powerful arms
> Moved by Your love, I'll stay close to Your heart
> Resting here with You

© Sally-Ann Fatkin 2008

The second page is from Christine Joyce, and has a circle which reads

Circle me Lord
Keep calm within
Keep storms without

Circle me Lord
Keep hope within
Despair without

Circle me Lord
Keep Strength within
Keep weakness out

Circle me Lord
Keep peace within
Keep turmoil out

What more can I say, other than My God Is A Great BIG God and He holds me in His hands. Many of you will know the song, but I enjoyed this version on YouTube as it made me smile. http://uk.youtube.com/watch?v=1mMZy05ooFY&feature=related

Be bold as you pray, my current needs are:-
- ❖ I will strongly sense God's amazing peace during this challenging period
- ❖ The operation will go well and without complications
- ❖ That the ileostomy can be reversed at a future date
- ❖ Pain will be controlled effectively during the healing process
- ❖ For Ginny and the family

"And the prayer offered in faith will make the sick person well, the Lord will raise him up. If he has sinned, he will be forgiven". James 5v15 sent to me by Nesiham Hukenek

Family news;

My father's day surgery to remove his skin cancer on the top of his head was successful. However, recovery is a little slower than he would like and some of you will be aware that my niece Kathryn had a kidney transplant on Wednesday 1st October. She came home on Sunday 5th and the kidney is working well and is being closely monitored

Blessings
Graham

(Mailing list 245)

12 October 2008

Tonight at 6.00pm I go into hospital for my major operation on Monday. However I have loads to do before then as I need to remove all my tools from our bedroom where, for the last two weeks, I have been fitting new bedroom furniture, a new bed as well as decorating the room and having a new carpet fitted after having the floorboards lifted to fit new lights in the kitchen below and additional power points. My project management skills have ensured all this has run to schedule and - just like work - finished on the last possible day. The grass also needs cutting plus a couple of trips to the rubbish tip.

Despite all that needs doing I went to church this morning where a friend asked Ginny whether we were going to have a quiet afternoon, walking by the Thames or something similar. Ginny explained all the jobs that I needed to complete and by the time we had got home, the phone had rung with offers of help with cutting the grass, trips to the tip and finishing off the bedroom. We are so blessed by belonging to a caring church and having such good friends as everything was finished by 4.45pm that afternoon.

Prayer focus for me in church today was great and I really sensed God's peace as I do now I have been admitted onto the ward. Remembered being humbled the night before when Simon Williams prayed at a dinner party we had at home and by Dave Robinson helping today and Martyn Ayliffe during the week.

Ginny and I walked around the hospital corridors for a while so we could spend some time together, came across the 24 hour vending machine where I bought a Mars bar and muffin to eat during the night as from 1.00am I would be nil by mouth with my operation being the last in the day.

Went to bed praying that Ginny, my boys Chris, Richard and Daniel would be OK.

14 October 2008 – Church Prayer Chain

Thank you for all your prayers, Graham is now out of intensive care and pain is under control. All went well and Graham is positive. He was strengthened by thinking of Job 5 v 9 which says *'He performs wonders that cannot be fathomed, miracles that cannot be counted'.*

17 October 2008 – Prayer Newsletter 21

Hi everyone,

Thank you for prayers, the operation has gone well and the cancer has been removed. However, recovery is slower then anticipated with much pain. Graham is now off the morphine and on different pain killers. He is starting to eat a little bit after a rough day yesterday and hasn't been sick today. He enjoyed many visitors today including two sons, daughter-in-law and wife.

He is still very positive which the nurses appreciate.

Please pray that tomorrow all drains and catheter will be removed and that pain will continue to be kept under control.

Ginny xx

18 October 2008

Today is a special day, it's my 51st birthday and also Chris's graduation day in London. In view of this the nurses allowed my family to visit me during the morning which isn't normally allowed. Ginny took the photo below which the boys very kindly put on Facebook for everyone to see but at least I'm smiling despite the hospital gown.

It was amazing to see Daniel who arrived the day before. He had sent me a text at 10.30am saying he had just finished his lectures for the week and was looking forward to the weekend. Then at 4.30pm when Chris and Rosie came to visit me, Chris said he had another present outside which wasn't wrapped. As I wondered what it could be, in he walked with Daniel who had travelled for 6 hours from Aberystwyth where he is at university.

A card from Chris included the following words:

5   "Every word of God is flawless;
    He is a shield to those who take refuge in Him.

Proverbs 30 v 5

And the words:
The God of all comfort will sustain and keep you. He will walk through every valley with you. He will stand before you in problems, storms and sorrow. He purchased peace on the cross. Be still and know that He is God.

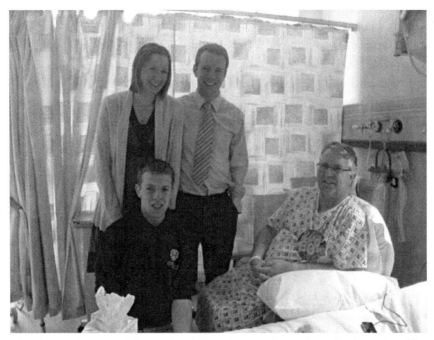

Standing Chris and Rosie Priddy – Sitting Daniel & Graham Priddy

19 October 2008 – Book of Encouragement

1   Answer me when I call to You,
    O my righteous God.
    Give me relief from my distress;
    be merciful to me and hear my prayer.
8   I will lie down and sleep in peace,
    for You alone, O LORD,
    make me dwell in safety.

Psalm 4 v 1 & 8

(Text from Lucy Tovey – Spring Harvest Chief Steward)

20 October 2008 – Book of Encouragement

29 He gives strength to the weary
    and increases the power of the weak.

Isaiah 40 v 29

(Text from Lucy Tovey – Spring Harvest Chief Steward)

23 October 2008 – Book of Encouragement

13 I can do everything through Him who gives me strength

Philippians 4 v 13

(Text from Rev David Priddy – Brother)

26 October 2008 – Church Prayer Chain

Please pray for Graham, he is in great pain and is vomiting. Pray
that the drugs he is receiving will be effective soon. He asks we pray for
the assurance of God's presence. Pray too, for a good night's sleep and
pray especially tonight for Ginny.

13 November 2008 – Book of Encouragement

3   Sing to Him a new song;
     play skilfully, and shout for joy.
4   For the word of the LORD is right and true;
     He is faithful in all He does.

Psalm 33 v 3 & 4

(Text from Rev David Priddy – Brother)

1 November 2008 – Prayer Newsletter 22

Hi everyone,

This is another little update from Ginny. Graham is loving it so much in hospital that he is about to start his fourth week in. He's seen the snow, wind and rain and is staying in the warm.

The great news is that all the cancer has been removed and all the polyps surrounding it were clear from cancer so that is done and dusted. He has had a rough three weeks managing pain and sickness. Only now is he managing to enjoy a little food which he needs for strength and healing. Sickness and indigestion pain now seem to have passed. He is managing to walk to the bathroom and to take a little slow walk up the corridor. His problem is the wound in his bottom which has had an infection and is still weeping and not healing. This is causing him a lot of pain and makes sitting almost impossible. He thanks everyone for their prayers, best wishes and messages on Facebook. Please continue to pray for healing in this wound that would bring him home.

I'm sure the nurses would be pleased to see him go now as he is becoming lippy and having awful jokes with them. He is positive about still being there and sees it as the best place.

Thank you everyone.

Ginny xx

2 November 2008 – Book of Encouragement

I have prayed for release from the enemy activity and for the healing hand of Jesus to touch the specific problem area and for a renewing of His peace.

(Text from David and Sue Partington – Woodley Baptist Church)

14th November 2008 – Prayer Newsletter 23

Hi Everyone

Last night, after 33 days, I left the security of the hospital and came home. It was a very emotional experience, so much so that as I walked into my lounge l just stood and cried for a while as it was all too much to take in.

I cannot really express in this update what I have been through, but it has been the most painful, emotional, draining experience of my life. However, I am so grateful for the birthday present my son Chris and his wife Rosie gave me of a small wooden cross which I often held onto when the pain was so intense, knowing that my Saviour would see me through that period. I also reflected that the pain I was experiencing was nothing compared to what Jesus suffered for me on that cross many years before so that I today could know Him personally.

I am extremely appreciative of all who visited me, 42 different people in all, some several times, some on good days, others who only stayed a few minutes because I couldn't cope with any longer, one couple I didn't even speak to but I knew they were there, you will never know how much these visits meant to me, knowing your care and love. Thank you for making the effort.

As for your prayer support, what can I say, other than God hears our cries and petitions as well as praise and thanks? He always answers; even if it's not how we expect and I had to learn that the answers were always in His time, not mine, leading to unexpected opportunities to share Jesus with others. The amount of prayers said for me must be many thousands by now, but every one counts.

For those unaware, the operation was more major than expected. The cancer was removed, along with 11 polyps surrounding that area, and as the cancer was so low down it was necessary to remove my rectum which has now been closed up. I also acquired an unusual infection which, when discovered, required additional antibiotics and me to be put into an isolation room for five days where visitors weren't even allowed to touch me and I was even told that I wasn't allowed to leave the confines of that room. My colostomy will now remain with me for the rest of my life which I have come to terms with.

Despite being home, my wound will still take a couple of months to fully heal, and it is this area that remains uncomfortable rather than painful. I will receive visits every day from the District Nurse who will clean the wound and change the dressing. I also have a small build up of fluid within my body which can't be drained because of its position, so the plan is to monitor this by CT scans every two weeks, trusting that it will disappear, rather than a further operation to remove it which my Registrar believes would be too much for me to cope with just now.

I'm not going to quote any scripture this time, as there are many to chose from that express my thanks to such a loving Father. However, I will leave you with this prayer that I took comfort from while in hospital which I think you will enjoy.

Heavenly Father,
You are God who watches day and night,
who never sleeps but cares for all You have created,
You ask me to be Your child, to look for You for everything.
I know You have the power, in which You organise the universe,
the power in which You involve me to play my part,
to play that part responsibly.

It is imperative that I trust You in all things,
that I recognise You are my maker, creator
    and Father, as being in love.
But in the essence of loves lies the power that conquers,
not by force but by sacrifice.
By calling me to be Your child,
You make me co-heir in serving my brother
    and sisters by sacrifice.

I know love is many things but, that sacrificial love is
    nearest in my quest to imitate the love of Jesus.
By His words and example, I have a life-pattern
    by which You want me to live.
And though His own did not understand Him
I have now the Holy Spirit to illuminate my mind
    and heart to lead me into all truth,
Help me, Heavenly Father,
to look to You for all things,
to trust in love,
to live by faith,
to be Your child.
Amen.

Current prayer requests are:
❖ Thank God for those who cared for me, and for
   progress so far
❖ My wound will continue to heal
❖ I can find comfortable ways to sit etc, without putting
   undue pressure on the wound.
❖ I will build up my strength but not put on the two
   stone I lost whilst in hospital.
❖ For safe travel as I spend the weekend in
   Fordingbridge with 17 other family members

Blessings
Graham

14 November 2008 – Book of Encouragement

Just to let you know that we are praying for you at this time of
disappointment. I came across these 'sayings' and hope they may be of
help. God be with you all.

Disappointments: His Appointments.

Disappointment: God's way of dimming the glamour of the world and deepening our ability to enjoy Him

(Psalms119:37).-Bill Gothard

Why art thou disquieted; because it happeneth not to thee according to thy wishes and desires? Who is he that hath everything according to his will? Neither I, nor thou, nor any man upon the earth.
-Thomas a Kempis

All I can say in this affair is that, however mysterious the leadings of Providence are, I have no doubt but they are superintended by an infinitely wise God.
-William Carey,
after he and his luggage were put ashore and he was denied passage
aboard the ship that was to take him as a missionary to India

I was reminded of this 'golden oldie' as well, especially the first line:

O love that wilt not let me go,
I rest my weary soul in Thee:
I give Thee back the life I owe,
That in Thine ocean depths its flow
May richer, fuller be.

O light that followest all my way,
I yield my flickering torch to Thee:
My heart restores its borrowed ray,
That in Thy sunshine's blaze its day
May brighter, fairer be.

O joy that seekest me through pain,
I cannot close my heart to Thee:
I trace the rainbow through the rain,
And feel the promise is not vain,
That morn shall tearless be

George Matheson (1842-1906)

(Email from Rev David Priddy – Brother)

16 November 2008 – Book of Encouragement

You are priceless in His eyes and forever in His care.

7   He pays even the greatest attention to
    you, down to the last detail

Luke 12 v 7

That's why the angels have never left you

(Card from Mary Hearn – Sister-in-Law)

20 November 2008 – Book of Encouragement

Jesus did not come to explain away suffering or to remove it. He
came to fill it with His presence.
Quote by Paul Louis Charles Claudel

(Card from Grace Hope – Woodley Baptist Church)

23 November 2008 – Book of Encouragement

14 Wait for the LORD;
   be strong and take heart
   and wait for the LORD.

Psalm 27 v 14

(Card from Pam Mullin – Woodley Baptist Church)

28 November 2008 – Prayer Newsletter 25

Greetings

During this week, I have been thinking a lot about Jesus, being the rock that has sustained me through what my District Nurse described as a very major operation. She tells me that I shouldn't underestimate what my body has been through, which was reinforced by a consultation with my Oncologist at the Cancer Unit on Wednesday.

Before I talk about the consultation, let me share with you a poem and some verses I have taken encouragement from this week from a card I received.

Jesus You are my Rock
However strong the winds
Of fortune may try to blow me off course,
Clinging to You, the Rock,
My rescue is assured.

In the safety of the Rock
I am invincible;
Though on my own
I would be as frail as grass,
Clinging to You, the Rock,
Will make me rock-like.

I am extremely grateful to my parents who laid the initial foundations of my Christian faith that has enabled me to hold onto all I believe during these months that have been the most difficult in my life. The words Jesus spoke in Luke 6 v 47 – 49 ring true. *'I will show you what he is like who comes to me and hears my words and puts them into practice. He is like a man building a house, who dug down deep and laid the foundation on rock. When a flood came, the torrent struck that house but could not shake it, because it was well built. But the one who hears my words and does not put them into practice is like a man who built a house on the ground without a foundation. The moment the torrent struck that house, it collapsed and its destruction was complete."*

Finally I declare that *'The LORD has become my fortress and my God the rock in whom I take refuge'. Psalm* 94 v 22 and in the words of Isaiah 26 v 4 which say *'Trust in the LORD forever, for the LORD, the LORD, is the Rock eternal'.*

OK, so what did the Oncologist say? Well, he reinforced that all the treatment to date had gone well with the tumour shrinking significantly prior to its removal. The operation, despite the complications afterwards, had gone well and, in view of the removal of surrounding areas and rectum, that no further traces of cancer are evident which should ensure that I should not encounter any further problems in years to come. He went on to say that under normal circumstances, within four weeks of the operation, as an extra precaution they like to do another eight weeks of chemotherapy. However, in my case, any benefits would be outweighed by the effects this would have on my body which hasn't yet recovered from the operation. In view of my overall progress, I shouldn't be concerned about this, but he would review this at my next appointment on 22nd December. Also that for the next three years, I would have six-monthly blood tests and scans just to ensure that the cancer does not return. His final words were I should have a great big smile on my face, so I walked out of the room with a great big smile on my face.

My next appointment is a CT scan next Friday afternoon to check the situation about the previous build up of fluid. My wound seems to be healing well and weather permitting I am able to walk a little further each day. I feel stronger as each week goes by. However I am not sleeping well and sense I'm still in hospital mode - bed at 11.00pm, up at 6.00am and waking every hour or two. My afternoon nap between 2.00pm and 3.00pm remains important to the healing process.

I enjoyed an outing to watch Reading play last Saturday despite arriving 25 minutes late due to my District Nurse failing to visit me as arranged in the morning. It was wonderful to get to church after 6 weeks away and I invited my wife out for a date, to the local garden centre for a coffee Sunday afternoon. I know - such a romantic!

Current prayer requests are:
- ❖ My wound will continue to heal without too much discomfort
- ❖ My sleeping pattern will return to normal
- ❖ The CT scan will show that the amount of fluid has reduced or disappeared
- ❖ I will build up my strength but not put on the 2 stone I lost whilst in hospital

Blessings
Graham

2 December 2008 – Book of Encouragement

9   But He said to me, "My grace is sufficient for you,
for My power is made perfect in weakness."
Therefore I will boast all the more
gladly about my weaknesses,
so that Christ's power may rest on me.
10 That is why, for Christ's sake,
I delight in weaknesses, in insults, in hardships,
in persecutions, in difficulties.
For when I am weak, then I am strong.

2 Corinthians 12 v 9 & 10

(Card from Lynne Gibson – Woodley Baptist Church)

3 December 2008 – Book of Encouragement

14 And we can be confidence that He will listen to us
   whenever we ask Him for anything in line with His will.
15 And if we know that He is listening
   when we make our requests,
   we can be sure that He will give us what we ask for.

1 John 5 v 14 & 15

(Book – 90 Minutes in Heaven)

3 December 2008 – Book of Encouragement

May those closest to me be drawn closer to you through me.
Amen.

(Book - Life Journey on Elijah Prophet of the lost)

5 December 2008 – Prayer Newsletter 26

Greetings

Today I return to the hospital for another CT scan, which basically
takes a lot of X-ray pictures of my body from different angles. These
pictures are fed into a computer which puts them together to give a
series of cross sections or 'slices' through the part of the body being
scanned. A very detailed picture of the inside of the body can be built
up in this way. Today's scan is to check whether the unexpected build
up of fluid has reduced or disappeared. This scan requires that I have
nothing to eat or drink 4 hours prior to the scan, and when I arrive at
the hospital I have to drink at least a litre of dilute barium dye in order
to accurately outline the stomach and intestines.

I'm hoping that my veins have recovered since my stay in hospital
as an intravenous injection (iodine based contrast medium) is required
during the scan as it shows the blood vessels in the body and outlines
certain structures to help the diagnosis. The result won't be known for

a few days but as I don't appear to have a temperature, I'm trusting that the result will be good news.

Shortly after I commenced these regular updates, which from individual feedback I know many have found encouraging and helpful, I decided that I would need to be totally honest about my feelings etc. This week in many respects has been good, and I have enjoyed talking at length with a number of visitors, acknowledging that I am so blessed with so many good friends. Today I even managed to walk to the local post office for the first time which for me is a real achievement and a goal I set myself when I came out of hospital. However, as the week ends, I have become fed up with evenings at home, feeling uncomfortable all of the time, having to wear a pad (large nappy) over my dressing, my stoma not being as regular as before and needing to get up three or four times during the night due to my legs aching and needing some exercise. I have also dwelt on the fact that I have been undergoing treatment now for eight months, knowing I still have a few months to go.

Last night my dear friend Lucy reminded me of Ephesians 2 v 21 & 22 *'In Him the whole building is joined together and rises to become a holy temple in the Lord. And in Him you too are being built together to become a dwelling in which God lives by His Spirit.'* And other scriptures referring to my body being a temple of God's Holy Spirit and how I needed to take good care of it.

This morning I looked at my favourite mug, given to me when I was in hospital by my brother, which has the following logo. 'STRENGTH FOR THE JOURNEY' and a Bible verse from Joshua 1 v 9 *"Have I not commanded you? Be strong and courageous. Do not be terrified; do not be discouraged, for the LORD your God will be with you wherever you go."*

Then I read Isaiah 57 v 10 which says *'You were wearied by all your ways, but you would not say, 'It is hopeless'. You found renewal of your strength, and so you did not faint'.*

Oh how I hate the way that when you are down, God provides the encouragement you need to carry on but then again, my God is an awesome God, which brings me to this week's song which can be found on YouTube. Do use the link below to look it up and forgive me when I say, 'it's an awesome clip' which you have to listen to.

http://www.youtube.com/watch?v=FjpuMWQRXAM The first words to the first verse and chorus of the song are below:

When He rolls up His sleeves,
He ain't just puttin' on the ritz.
Our God is an awesome God.
There is thunder in His footsteps
And lightning in His fists.
Our God is an awesome God.

Chorus

Our God is an awesome God.
He reigns from heaven above;
With wisdom, power and love,
Our God is an awesome God.

© Rich Mullins 1988 BMG Songs, Inc

To finish, I have recently spoken to a couple of people about how I discovered I had bowel cancer as they have been concerned about their own health and last week I learned of a work colleague who has just commenced treatment for bowel cancer. In view of what I have been through, I thought it was time to provide some information about bowel cancer, bearing in mind I was told that my cancer could have been growing for ten years prior to my visit to my GP for treatment.

So what are the symptoms - noting that not everyone will have symptoms and the symptoms may vary? The most common symptoms to look out for are:

❖ A persistent change in bowel habit especially going more often or looser for several weeks;
❖ Bleeding from the bottom without any obvious reason;
❖ Abdominal pain, especially if severe;
❖ A lump in your tummy.
❖ Unexplained anaemia causing tiredness or
❖ Weight loss.

Please remember that most of these symptoms will not be cancer. If you have one or more of these symptoms for more than four to six weeks you should go and see your GP. More information can be found at http://www.beatingbowelcancer.org/index.html

Current prayer requests are:
- ❖ My wound will continue to heal without too much discomfort
- ❖ My sleeping pattern will return to normal
- ❖ I will feel more positive in the weeks to come as recovery and treatment continues

Remember the true meaning of Christmas.

Blessings
Graham

8 December 2008 – Book of Encouragement

5 "That I may know how to sustain the weary one with a word,
   He awakens me morning by morning.
   He awakens my ear to listen as a disciple.
6 The Lord has opened my ear and I was not disobedient,
   Nor did I turn back".

Isaiah 50 VV 4 - 5

(Email from Jonathan and Alison Frater – Spring Harvest Steward)

12 December 2008 – Prayer Newsletter 27

Season's greetings,
I didn't sleep that well on Wednesday night, it may have been the excitement of the Christmas meals on Thursday (work event) and Friday (Church Men's Breakfast group). However, I found myself thanking God in the early hours for all His blessings I have encountered in my

life, including health situation, family, friends, employment, my faith, material goods - to mention a few.

Some people have been amazed at how well I have dealt with my illness. Bearing in mind I couldn't do hospitals, watch medical soaps, or even watch an injection in a movie prior to my first consultation, I am amazed too, other than I put it all down to claiming the promises of God, the power of prayer and your commitment to praying for me and my family. This update is now sent to 296 people around the world, and I know it is forwarded at work to a number of colleagues as well as being aware that some churches with whom I have no personal connection have also committed to pray for my recovery. Isn't the Christian community wonderful to be a part of?

One of the things I have never done is to question God as to why this has happened to me, but if I had, the answer was written on a piece of paper I picked up at random from a basket, following my first operation in the prayer room at Spring Harvest which read, *'Because I love you with an everlasting love'* taken from Jeremiah 31 v 3. This has since been reinforced by another verse I read this week from Isaiah 43 v 4 *'Since you are precious and honoured in My sight, and because I love you,'* Aren't these verses fantastic?

Thanks for all your prayers in the last week, particularly as I had asked you to pray that 'I would feel more positive'. Your prayers have certainly been answered in this area. Also, despite the fact that it took a couple of attempts to find a useable vein, the CT scan seemed to go OK. However, I do have to wait until 22nd December to get the results.

My main wound seems to be healing nicely, however this week my District Nurse discovered that a new smaller wound has opened up which concerned me slightly as it appears to be a step backwards. However, a card on our fridge, again from my dear friend Lucy reads: 'Have Faith – Trust – Rest Assured', plus a verse from Romans 15:13 *'May the God of hope fill you with all joy and peace as you trust in Him, so that you may overflow with hope by the power of the Holy Spirit'.* So I have to ask myself - what's there to be concerned about?

Sorry, no songs or poems this week, but two more scriptures. The first from Jonathan Frater (Spring Harvest Steward) Isaiah 50 v 4-5 *'that I may know how to sustain the weary with a word. Morning by morning He wakens, wakens my ear to listen as a disciple. The Lord GOD has opened my ear, and I was not disobedient, I did not turn backward.'*

The second from Lorraine Hotson, which I believe is for us all in this difficult economic climate as we look to the future Jeremiah 29 v 11 *"For I know the plans I have for you," declares the LORD, "plans to prosper you and not to harm you, plans to give you hope and a future'.* Lorraine, I then read further into verses 12 – 14 which say *"Then you will call upon me and come and pray to me, and I will listen to you. You will seek me and find me when you seek me with all your heart. I will be found by you," declares the LORD'* ☺. Again fantastic verses.

My next trip to the Hospital is Monday 15th for a blood test prior to my clinic appointment on 22nd December.

Current prayer requests are:
❖ My wounds will continue to heal
❖ My sleeping pattern will return to normal
❖ I will be totally recovered and 100% fit prior to Spring Harvest week 3 in Minehead. ☺

Remember the true meaning of Christmas

Blessings
Graham

22 December 2008 – Prayer Newsletter 28

Season's greetings,

Well, in a few days time we will be celebrating Christmas, the most significant birthday of all time and I pray that God will pour out His richest blessing on you as you enjoy the plans you have made. Christmas can be a busy time, but please take time to reflect on the following poems, the first published in my church magazine, the second by Elizabeth Tuttle.

If you look for Me at Christmas,
you won't need a special star -

I'm no longer just in Bethlehem,
I'm right there where you are.

You may not be aware of Me
amid the celebrations ~
You'll have to look beyond the stores
and all the decorations.

But if you take a moment
from your list of things to do
And listen to your heart, you'll find
I'm waiting there for you.

You're the one I want to be with,
you're the reason that I came,
And you'll find Me in the stillness
as I'm whispering your name.

Love Jesus

Church Magazine

Humble King
You who are mightiest
The King of all Kings,
Do not come with great pomp
You come to me in the gentle breeze
like a shadow
falling over me
quietly
in the stillness of my heart.
If I expect You, Jesus,
You will be there.

© Elizabeth Tuttle

Jeremiah 29 v 13 reads *"You will seek me and find me when you seek me with all your heart"*

This morning I saw my Oncologist at the Cancer Unit who gave me some excellent news; The CT scan I had on 5th December showed that the previous build up of fluid has reduced. It had been decided that a further 8 week course of chemotherapy will not be necessary in view of the success of previous treatments. The blood test results were absolutely fine.

As you can imagine, I am rejoicing with this excellent news and am reminded of, Psalm 103 v 1 – 5 which reads, *'Praise the LORD, O my soul; all my inmost being, praise His holy name. Praise the LORD, O my soul, and forget not all His benefits - who forgives all your sins and heals all your diseases, who redeems your life from the pit and crowns you with love and compassion, who satisfies your desires with good things so that your youth is renewed like the eagle's.'*

And also of a hymn my father sent me back in August,

Rejoice! The Lord is King.
Your Lord and King adore;
Mortals, give thanks and sing,
And triumph evermore:
Lift up your heart, lift up your voice:
Rejoice; again I say, rejoice.

Charles Wesley (1707-88)

The above are clear answers to your many prayers, so I thank you and God for your valuable prayer support.

Current prayer requests are:
- ❖ My Christmas plans will not be hampered by waiting around for District Nurses to arrive to change my dressing
- ❖ My wounds will continue to heal
- ❖ My sleeping pattern will return to normal
- ❖ I will be totally recovered and 100% fit prior to Spring Harvest week 3 in Minehead. ☺

Moving into 2009, I plan to claim and take comfort from these words in Jeremiah 30 v 17 *"But I will restore you to health and heal your wounds,"* declares the LORD.

And before I finish a little Christmas laughter on the theme of 'Why Jesus is Better Than Santa Claus'.

Santa Claus lives at the North Pole...
JESUS is everywhere.

Santa Claus comes but once a year...
JESUS is an ever present help.

Santa Claus fills your stockings with goodies...
JESUS supplies all your needs.

While Santa Claus puts gifts under your tree...
JESUS became our gift and died on a tree.

Sorry for that, but it is Christmas.

My next update will be in the New Year, so remember the true meaning of Christmas, enjoy yourself and I pray that God will reveal Himself to you at a deeper level in 2009.

Blessings
Graham

23 December 2008 – Book of Encouragement

I have just been reading back your prayer newsletters and am amazed yet again by God's goodness. He never promised us an easy problem free life, but He has assured us that He is ALWAYS with us.

Thank you for sharing your journey. It has been a blessing to so many. I was thinking on Sunday, when you were in the foyer, how far you had come. In bad times God has assured me that He has me in the hollow of His hand, and He delights in me. Your testimony is the same. Praise, praise Him.

(Email from Judy Breavington – Woodley Baptist Church)

23 December 2008 – Book of Encouragement

11 For I know the plans I have for you," declares the LORD,
  "plans to prosper you and not to harm you,
  plans to give you hope and a future

Jeremiah 29 v 11

(Email from Lorraine Hotson – Woodley Baptist Church

1 January 2009

With 2008 being a year of various treatments and operations, 2009 will be the year that the healing process will be completed apart from a few on-going check ups and scans. I came across the following verse which I'm going to claim as my verse for 2009.

17 "But I will restore you to health and heal your wounds," declares the LORD.

Jeremiah 30 v 17

3 January 2009 – Prayer Newsletter 29

May I wish you all a very Happy New Year and I trust that you enjoyed the plans you made over the Christmas period.

As for the Priddy's we had a wonderful time celebrating the birth of Jesus with the District Nurse arriving early enough on Christmas morning to enable us all to get to Church. Yes, it seemed I was important enough to still have the District Nurse visit every day over the Christmas period, but this didn't interfere with our plans (more answers to prayer). Having said that, as I use the spare bedroom as the 'medical room', on occasions Richard and Daniel had to get up earlier than they liked when the District Nurse arrived before 9.00am.

I made a couple of unplanned visits to the hospital over the Christmas period, one on Christmas Eve and another a few days later due to a problem I was having with my stoma, however this is now all sorted. In my last update, I stated that moving into 2009, I plan to claim and take comfort from these words in Jeremiah 30 v 17 *"But I will restore you to health and heal your wounds,"* declares the LORD and this verse is very much at the forefront of my mind especially because, as I write this, I am not feeling great. This is due to the fact that for the last few days I have suffered with a stiff neck and shoulder and have now caught a bad cold in addition to the normal discomfort from my dressing.

As I mentioned dressings, positive news is that my wounds are continuing to heal nicely and are now clean on most days. This has meant that I can stop wearing a pad (large nappy) over my main dressing. I now have a much smaller pad which, whilst still uncomfortable, is significantly better.

Current prayer requests are:
- ❖ My cold and stiffness will quickly pass.
- ❖ My wounds will continue to heal
- ❖ I will be totally recovered and 100% fit prior to Spring Harvest week 3 in Minehead. ☺

Happy New Year.

Blessings
Graham

"But I will restore you to health and heal your wounds," declares the LORD. - Jeremiah 30 v 17

3 January 2009 – Book of Encouragement

7   The Lord is good, a refuge in time of trouble,
     He cares for those who trust Him

Nahum 1 v 7

(Email from Rev David Priddy – Brother)

4th January 2009 – Sunday Evening Service on prayer - My testimony

I have been asked to share my experiences about the Power of Prayer, God's Faithfulness of Answers to Prayer in my life during 2008

Many of you have been following my journey but like most people here, I consider myself to be an ordinary Christian, struggling at times to follow what I read in the Bible and teaching here. However a year ago, for the first time in my life, I was to encounter some serious health issues, as after a number of examinations and scans, it was confirmed on 20th March that I had bowel cancer although I had known something was wrong months before.

Throughout that day I very much felt God's peace as never before which I'm sure is a direct result of the prayers of a few that I had shared my situation with.

Despite being a person who keeps most things to himself it was clear to me that I would need to depend on God more than ever before, especially as I couldn't cope with anything medical. So as my treatment began, I knew that the power of prayer would be essential to helping me face the future and overcome this cancer and so my first prayer chain was carefully written, encouraging people to be bold as they prayed in view of the seriousness of my condition and the major operation I faced. It read:-

'Please pray for Graham and the family as Graham has the first part of his treatment for bowel cancer with colostomy surgery this evening. Pray boldly that the surgery will be successful and without complications and that Graham will be able to adjust quickly to this life style change. Please pray for peace for Graham, Ginny and the family.'

The follow up prayer chain a few days later on 3rd April read:-

'Thank you for your prayers for Graham who is progressing well after yesterday's surgery. Please pray for an ongoing experience of God's peace for Graham, Ginny and family as recovery and treatment continue.'

Knowing that prayer was so important, and to ensure it was focused on my real needs, I started sending out regular prayer updates so that prayer could be focused on real needs rather than being of a general nature.

I will now read back some extras from these updates highlighting answers I have seen.

In my first prayer update following my first major operation I stated that:

I have been greatly supported and encouraged by prayer support and the medical staff were impressed with my excellent progress. In fact the day after my discharge, at the amazement of many, I travelled to Spring Harvest at Minehead, again an answer to prayer.

To me Spring Harvest was important, however this time it was to be a family holiday, something we had not done before. During the week I visited the Prayer House where I gave my cancer over to God, saying whilst I wanted to be totally healed, I wanted God to use it for His good. This was not an easy prayer for me, but one I have not regretted as God has answered and is continuing to answer this prayer.

How?

By my personal growth and dependence on Jesus

Expanding my gifting of encouragement to others

My boldness is sharing my faith with others

Other answers to Prayer:

1 September update

I quoted Psalm 106 v 1, which says "Give thanks to the LORD, for He is good; His love endures forever". I quote this as encouragement to you all who have faithfully prayed for me as the hospital confirmed this morning that the chemotherapy & radiotherapy has had a significant impact on reducing the tumour when the treatment normally only has a 60% chance of success.

5 September update

My operation will be on Monday 13th October - being admitted the afternoon before. However, once again your prayers have been answered as this date means that Ginny and I will be able to move Daniel to Aberystwyth University on 20th September. The operation date is a month later than originally stated by my Consultant.

1 November update

Thank you for your prayers, the operation has gone well and the great news is that all the cancer has been removed and all 11 polyps surrounding it were clear from cancer, but have also been removed so that is done and dusted.

14 November update

As for your prayer support, what can I say, other than God hears our cries and petitions as well as praise and thanks? He always answers, even if it's not how we expect and I had to learn that the answers were always in His time not mine, leading to unexpected opportunities to share Jesus with others. The amount of prayers said for me must be many thousands by now, but every one counts.

One opportunity of sharing the power of prayer was when my condition deteriorated after three weeks and the Outreach Intensive Care Nurse helped me word a prayer chain whilst I was on the phone to Ginny. Whilst he wasn't a church goer, he acknowledged that he had seen the power of answered prayer in his job.

24 December update

This morning I saw my Oncologist at the Cancer Unit who gave me some excellent news;

the CT scan I had on 5th December showed that the previous build up of fluid has reduced, no further scans needed for this.

It had been decided that a further 8 week course of chemotherapy will not be necessary in view of the success of previous treatments.

The blood test results were absolutely fine.

As you can imagine, I am rejoicing with this excellent news and clear answers to prayer.

Just before I finish let me share this prayer from my June 27th update that is so relevant

I do not know what life may hold,
if good or ill I'll see
what twist and turns may yet unfold,
what trials yet might be?

I cannot say if light will shine
or darkness fall once more,
what destiny might still be mine,
what future lies in store?

But even if the way is tough
and storms begin to blow,
the gales prove strong, the water rough,
one thing, Lord, still I know:

That You'll be there, supporting me,
a faithful, loving guide –
a constant help who will not fail
to strengthen and provide.

I have no need to ask for more
nor any cause to fear;
whatever life may hold for me

I know that you'll be near.

To conclude:-

Some words from 1 Peter 5 v 6 & 7
Humble yourselves, therefore under God's mighty hand that He may lift you up, Cast all your anxiety on Him because He cares for you.

And as I have done this, and enlisted the prayer support of many others,

God has remained at the centre,
God has held my hand,
God has lifted me up,
God has carried me,
God has grown me,
God has healed me,
God has enabled me to be an encouragement to others,

9 January 2009 – Prayer Newsletter 30

This has not been a fun week, as since my last update my bad cold developed further to the stage that I spent 2.5 days in bed and had sickness and diarrhoea. At times God seemed far away as this wasn't how I planned to start 2009, having chosen Jeremiah 30 v 17 as my verse for the year. *"But I will restore you to health and heal your wounds," declares the LORD'*. So was God being funny or was He trying to tell me something?

Sadly I missed the 24 hour prayer event at church where at its conclusion I was scheduled to give my testimony about answered prayer during 2008.

Just prior to writing this, I listened to the recording of that service where Judith Breavington pretended to be me and read out some of what I was going to share (text available on request). Listening to this and hearing aloud God's continued faithfulness in answering prayer in my life, remembering what I have been through brought me to tears (audio file attached to email)

At the start of that service they sang the song below called "What a Faithful God Have I" and I can think of no better song to share in this prayer letter as it's an excellent reminder of God's faithfulness in my life. Below is the first verse and chorus but the full version can be found at the following YouTube link ihttp://uk.youtube.com/watch?v =gLEgyKpzyUw&feature=related

Lord, I come before Your throne of grace;
I find rest in Your presence,
And fullness of joy.
In worship and wonder I behold Your face,
Singing what a faithful God have I.

Chorus
What a faithful God have I,
What a faithful God.
What a faithful God have I,
Faithful in every way.

© Robert and Dawn Critchley, 1989 Thankyou Music

This Monday it will be exactly three months ago that I went into hospital for my operation and I am beginning to believe what the doctors told me at the outset that recovery could take six months. The length of recovery I am beginning to find frustrating with its limitations of lack of movement and the freedom to get out and do 'normal' things, especially now Christmas is over.

Linked to this, I recently finished a book called '90 Minutes in Heaven' by Don Piper. Don was killed by an 18-wheeler truck and went to heaven, then as the title suggests, 90 minutes later, he returned to life and the book tells of his road to healing, including being confined to bed for 13 months and having to cope with intense pain and ongoing limitation.

One section of his book that touched me was when Don highlighted that God showed him to be grateful for all the things he could do, and to stop moaning about the things he couldn't do. At times this is something I need to remind myself of and I remember whilst I was in hospital, how often I thanked God for being able to carry out such routine tasks, such as walking to the bathroom, cleaning my teeth, or pouring a glass of water, which at the time was so difficult. Oh how we take so much for granted.

Maybe I need to take comfort in Romans 5 v 3 to 5 which says, *3 'Not only so, but we also rejoice in our sufferings, because we know that suffering produces perseverance; 4 perseverance, character; and character, hope. 5 And hope does not disappoint us, because God has poured out His love into our hearts by the Holy Spirit, whom He has given us.'*

Whilst on the subject of suffering, this morning I asked my District Nurse to try and find ways of giving my bum a rest from the continued bombardment of sticky dressings which, in my opinion, give me more discomfort that the wound itself. Having mentioned the wound, the Nurse took a swab this morning in order to establish whether I have an infection that needs additional treatment.

Current prayer requests are:
- ❖ If the wound is infected that an effective drug will be found to treat it and to aid continued healing without adverse side effects
- ❖ A more comfortable way of dressing the wound will be found
- ❖ I will be totally recovered and 100% fit prior to Spring Harvest week 3 in Minehead. ☺

Blessings
Graham

"But I will restore you to health and heal your wounds," declares the LORD. - Jeremiah 30 v 17

16 January 2009 – Prayer Newsletter 31

Firstly let me apologise for the audio file I sent out last week, it would appear that some people were able to play it, others weren't. I trust you didn't waste hours trying to make it work as you stared at my photo.

Like last week, this week hasn't been fun due to the fact that the stiffness in my arm and neck has been more painful than the wounds from my operation. I put this down to spending too much time sitting on the sofa using my laptop and I realised that this has slowly developed into a bad habit, taking me away from other things such as reading and listening to music. In fact it was a song by Matt Redman called 'Show me the way of the cross once again' that brought things back into focus. I have listened to this repeatedly during the week as the words are so relevant to me at this time, requiring me to review my own life and to respond.

The words are to the first verse are but for full lyrics follow the YouTube link for this song at http://www.youtube.com/watch?v=n41DeS5zm24

Show me the way of the cross once again
Denying myself for the love that I've gained
Everything's You now, everything's changed,
It's time You had my whole life;
You can have it all.

© Matt Redman, 1996 Thankyou Music

Once again, I thank you for your continued prayer support and I encourage you all to join me in thanking God as two of the prayer focus points from last week have clearly been answered this week. The swab taken last Friday to establish whether I have an infection that needs additional treatment proved negative. Not only that, but one wound has closed over and the other wound is much cleaner this week with less blood showing on the dressing. A more comfortable way of dressing the wound has been found and my bum is no longer bombarded with sticky dressings

The Psalms offer much inspiration when it comes to praising God and I will quote from Psalm 40 v 5 in light of Him answering your prayers. *'Lord God, You have piled high Your marvellous deeds and thoughtfulness towards us; none can begin to compare with You! I will make known what You have done to all, speaking of blessings beyond number.'*

And also from Psalm 89 v 1 & 2 '*1 I will sing of the LORD'S great love forever; with my mouth I will make Your faithfulness known through all generations. 2 I will declare that Your love stands firm forever, that You established Your faithfulness in heaven itself.*'

I also managed to drive my car for the first time since my operation three months ago and it was lovely to get a little bit of independence back into my life. I drove to my office where I spent 2.5 hours speaking with colleagues. However, the main reason for the visit was to hand over my next medical certificate as on Monday my Doctor signed me off work until 12th April 2009, which made me realise that when the Doctor told me at the outset that it may take 6 months to recover from the operation, he was probably right. I remain thankful to God for having such an understanding and supportive employer who are treating me so well during my illness.

Current prayer requests are:
- ❖ My painful neck and arm will be healed quickly
- ❖ My wounds will continue to heal
- ❖ I will be totally recovered and 100% fit prior to Spring Harvest week 3 in Minehead. ☺

Blessings
Graham

"But I will restore you to health and heal your wounds," declares the LORD. - Jeremiah 30 v 17

16 January 2009 – Prayer Book of Encouragement

3   Lord God, You have piled high Your marvellous deeds
    and thoughtfulness towards us,
    none can begin to compare with You.
    I will make known what You have done to all,
    speaking of blessings beyond number.

Psalm 40 v 3

1   I will sing of the Lord's great love forever,
    with my mouth I will make Your faithfulness
    known through all generations.
2   I will declare that Your love stands firm forever,
    That You establish Your faithfulness in heaven itself

Psalm 89 v 1 & 2

(Book – Nick Fawcett – How to Pray)

22 January 2009 – Church Prayer Chain

Graham was admitted to the Royal Berkshire Hospital very early
this morning with severe abdominal pain. He has been treated with
intravenous fluids. Please pray that he will respond to this and that his
vomiting will cease. Pray too, that he will have no further problems.

26 January 2009 – Book of Encouragement

9   "Have I not commanded you?
    Be strong and courageous.
    Do not be terrified; do not be discouraged,
    for the LORD your God will be with you wherever you go."

Joshua 1 v 9

(Text from Rev David Priddy – Brother) This has become a major
verse for me in recent days as it provides so much encouragement
knowing that God is with me wherever I go.

28 January 2009 – Book of Encouragement

1 'Answer me when I call to You,
O my righteous God.
Give me relief from my distress;
be merciful to me and hear my prayer'.

Psalm 4 v 1

(Text from Rev David Priddy – Brother)

31 January 2009 – Prayer Newsletter 32

It's good to be home again; however most people reading this will be unaware that I was admitted into hospital via ambulance in the early hours of Thursday 22nd January after calling the night doctor as I was suffering with severe stomach pains.

On arrival I was given some pain relief, then put on a drip for the next 48 hours and told I wasn't allowed to eat or drink anything until further notice. At 8.30am Friday morning I had a CT scan. However when the Consultant reviewed this, she wanted a second opinion before confirming what was wrong. Despite the second opinion not being obtained until Sunday evening I was allowed to start having fluids such as soups from lunchtime.

Monday morning my Registrar saw me and advised that I had what is known as adhesions (sticky bowel) resulting from scar tissue which can occur after major bowel surgery. He went on to remind me that the surgery I had had was one of the biggest operations they do.

Tuesday lunchtime I progressed to soft foods, then every day since Wednesday morning I was advised I could go home after lunch, assuming that my stoma had started working again. Finally on Friday afternoon, as I was no longer in pain I was allowed home despite my stoma still not being active and advised that the strong laxative I am taking should resolve the problem over the weekend.

On a positive side, and I think you all know me well enough to know that I will always look for the positives, it was good to meet up with lots of nurses and other staff who remembered me from my previous stays, whilst we all appreciated that it would have been better for me not to be in hospital.

During my stay, I received the following two scripture verses from my brother David which provided encouragement in my hours of need.

Joshua 1 v 9 *"Have I not commanded you? Be strong and courageous. Do not be terrified; do not be discouraged, for the LORD your God will be with you wherever you go."*

Psalm 4 v 1 *'Answer me when I call to You, O my righteous God. Give me relief from my distress; be merciful to me and hear my prayer'.*

Isn't our God amazing? With the frustration of not being allowed home, I received a text from my Church Elder Pete on Wednesday which said 'enjoy the fruit of Patience', only to receive another text from my dear friend Lucy saying that a friend in her housegroup had just prayed that 'I would be graced with Patience'. Neither of these people knows each other and at this stage in my recovery I certainly need to experience more of God's gift of Patience as I must be careful not to overdo things now I am feeling better within myself.

Current prayer requests are:
- ❖ The laxatives work and my stoma starts working properly again.
- ❖ My wounds will continue to heal
- ❖ I will be totally recovered and 100% fit prior to Spring Harvest week 3 in Minehead. ☺

Blessings
Graham

"But I will restore you to health and heal your wounds," declares the LORD. - Jeremiah 30 v 17

6 February 2009 – Prayer Newsletter 33

Hi Everyone,

I know a lot of people are very encouraged by reading my updates and I pray that this week will be no exception as I have always been open about treatments and feelings. However I have to say as I eventually got out of bed this morning, I'm fed up feeling uncomfortable with accompanying pain and various noises within my digestive system which often sound like pulling the plug out of the sink and the water draining away.

As the week ends, despite my stoma working overtime from the laxatives on Monday/Tuesday, nothing appears to have changed. This has also meant that I have been effectively housebound which is depressing as before this setback I was becoming a little more independent.

Interestingly enough, my Bible reading notes this morning read 'We all have tough days – or months – or years – when life batters us into emotional numbness. The challenge is to keep plodding on. The scripture I quoted last week from Joshua 1 v 9 remains relevant "Have I not commanded you? Be strong and courageous. Do not be terrified; do not be discouraged, for the LORD your God will be with you wherever you go."

My favourite cheer me up song on my iPod is one sung by Tim Hughes called "Hey Lord, O Lord". It's a real sing-a-long song and I was caught on more than one occasion singing along to it in hospital to the amusement of those around me. It's not a difficult song to remember as you will see from the words below:-

Hey Lord (Hey Lord), O Lord (O Lord)
Hey Lord (Hey Lord) You know what we need
Hey Lord (Hey Lord), O Lord (O Lord)
Hey Lord (Hey Lord) You know what we need

Lala lalalalalala...

Jesus (Jesus), You're the One (You're the One)
You set my heart (You set my heart) on fire
Jesus (Jesus), You're the One (You're the One)
You set my heart (You set my heart) on fire

Lala lalalalalala...

© Tim Hughes

Whilst God remains close to me and I to Him, I am reminded of a card given me by a work colleague Brigid entitled 'Footprints in the Sand' by Mary Stevenson. This will of course be known to many but it's a good reminder of God's faithfulness, picking up verses in Hebrews 13, 5 & 6 5'........*and be content with what you have, for God has said, "I will never leave you or abandon you." 6 hence we can confidently say, "The Lord is my helper; I will not be afraid. What can anyone do to me?"* I know during my illness God has needed to carry me several times whilst others prayed.

Here are the words;
One night I dreamed I was walking along
    the beach with the Lord.
Many scenes from my life flashed across the sky.
In each scene I noticed footprints in the sand.
Sometimes there were two sets of footprints,
other times there were one set of footprints.

This bothered me because I noticed
that during the low periods of my life,
when I was suffering from anguish, sorrow or defeat,
I could see only one set of footprints.

So I said to the Lord,
"You promised me Lord,
that if I followed You,
You would walk with me always.

But I have noticed that during the most trying
    periods of my life there have only been one
set of footprints in the sand.
Why, when I needed You most,
You have not been there for me?"

The Lord replied,
"The times when you have seen only one
        set of footprints in the sand,
is when I carried you."

© Mary Stevenson 1936

I found on YouTube, a song by Leona Lewis which picks up the theme of this poem. The link is http://www.youtube.com/watch?v=NG2ZLWeh3ks

To end on a positive note, my wounds continue to heal nicely, in fact they have now joined together into a single, longer but shallower wound with very little blood loss. This is really good news but still requires the District Nurse to call each day.

Current prayer requests are:
- ❖ My digestive system will start working normally again.
- ❖ I will enjoy the forthcoming week.
- ❖ The excellent progress with healing my wound will continue.
- ❖ I will be totally recovered and 100% fit prior to Spring Harvest week 3 in Minehead.☺

Blessings
Graham

"But I will restore you to health and heal your wounds," declares the LORD. - Jeremiah 30 v 17

6 February 2009 – Book of Encouragement

17 For our light and momentary troubles are
    achieving for us an eternal glory
    that far outweighs them all

2 Corinthians 4 v 17

(Email from David Partington – Woodley Baptist Church)

12 February 2009 – Church Prayer Chain

Please pray for Ginny and Graham. Graham was readmitted to the Royal Berkshire Hospital overnight with severe vomiting and abdominal pain. Pray that the treatment he is receiving will relieve the symptoms. Pray too for patience and that surgery will be avoided.

16 February 2009 – Church Prayer Chain

Graham will be going to theatre at 2pm for major surgery. Please pray that all the recent problems will be resolved and for the skill of the surgeon and his team. Pray for both Ginny and Graham that they will know the peace and strength of God's love throughout this time.

17 February 2009 – Church Prayer Chain

Graham thanks you all for your prayers and is now comfortable after a four hour operation to remove some infected bowel. Pain relief is working well and some tubes should be removed tomorrow. Please continue to pray for a speedy recovery without infection.

23 February 2009 – Church Prayer Chain

Graham is to have his catheter removed at 6am tomorrow. Please pray that this is successful and for his peace of mind as there were problems when this was done before.

3 March 2009

This morning during the doctors' rounds, my Senior Surgeon asked if she could come back later in the day and discuss the results of the biopsy, however there was nothing to worry about. As I was still extremely weak, I asked that Ginny be present and we agreed that 5.00pm would be a convenient time.

At 5.00pm my Senior Surgeon had been called to do an emergency operation so instead my Registrar met with Ginny and me. He explained that the 30cm section of bowel that had been removed to their surprise was full of cancer cells. He went on to explain that there was nothing more they could do. This was a real shock to us, as it was to the whole medical team. He then left Ginny and me alone with the curtains closed so we could have some time alone together.

Ginny cried most of the night and I slept OK but cried after reading and listening to the following, appreciating that life is clearly going to take a different course than I had planned:-

1 As the deer pants for streams of water,
   so my soul pants for You, O God.
2 My soul thirsts for God, for the living God.
   When can I go and meet with God?
3 My tears have been my food day and night,
   while men say to me all day long,
   "Where is Your God?"
4 These things I remember
   as I pour out my soul:
   how I used to go with the multitude,
   leading the procession to the house of God,
   with shouts of joy and thanksgiving
   among the festive throng.
5 Why are you downcast, O my soul?
   Why so disturbed within me?
   Put your hope in God,
   for I will yet praise Him,
   my Saviour and my God.
6 My soul is downcast within me;
   therefore I will remember you
   from the land of the Jordan,
   the heights of Hermon—from Mount Mizar.
7 Deep calls to deep
   in the roar of your waterfalls;
   all your waves and breakers
   have swept over me.
8 By day the LORD directs His love,
   at night His song is with me—
   a prayer to the God of my life.

9   I say to God my Rock,
       "Why have you forgotten me?
       Why must I go about mourning,
       oppressed by the enemy?"
10 My bones suffer mortal agony
       as my foes taunt me,
       saying to me all day long,
       "Where is your God?"
11 Why are you downcast, O my soul?
       Why so disturbed within me?
       Put your hope in God,
       for I will yet praise Him,
       my Saviour and my God.

Psalm 42 v 1 – 11

Song sung by Robin Mark based on Psalm 42
As the deer pants for the water,
So my soul longs after You.
You alone are my heart's desire,
And I long to worship You.

You alone are my strength, my shield,
To You alone may my spirit yield -
You alone are my heart's desire,
And I long to worship You.

See YouTube link for full lyrics at http://www.youtube.com/
watch?v=YY0t6_V1OqQ

4 March 2009

This morning during the doctors' rounds, my Senior Surgeon apologised that she had been unable to speak with Ginny and me as planned yesterday and that her Registrar had broken the news about my cancer having returned. I could tell by the look in her eyes that the news had in fact been a real surprise to everyone as previous blood tests and scans had shown that I had responded well to all treatments and the cancer had gone.

However, she went on to explain that it wasn't as bleak as we had been told as Mr Farouk meant that there were no more operations they could do as the cancer was on the lining of my abdomen. She then explained that tomorrow the Oncologist would see me to discuss further chemotherapy as a way of containing the cancer.

5 March 2009

Ginny arrived on the ward at 10.15am so that she could be with me when the Oncologist saw me. He explained that in a few weeks' time, when I have rebuilt my strength and recovered from my operation, I will commence a six month course of chemotherapy, being treated over a 48 hour period every two weeks. The aim of this is to contain the cancer and we have been advised that the six months following this course of chemotherapy will be critical.

We both felt significantly better after this chat and we began to make plans as to who we need to tell about the cancer returning and in what order, with our children being top of the list. This means that I shall have to be a little selective in my next few Prayer Newsletters which makes me feel a little uncomfortable in view of being so honest in them, but on this occasion I know that family must come first and that, in time, people will understand.

7 March 2009 – Prayer Newsletter 34

I'm home at last; however some of you will be unaware of events since my last prayer letter of 6th February 2009.

When my District Nurse arrived on Saturday she insisted I visited the weekend on call doctor at the hospital as she was unhappy with how I looked as my stoma had stopped working again. Following this visit, I was prescribed increased laxatives which seemed to do the trick a few days later. However the discomfort within my digestive system remained so that I spent most of the next three days in bed.

Wednesday evening 11th February, after being violently sick, I again visited the out-of-hours doctor at the hospital who had no hesitation in admitting me via the A & E department. I was subsequently placed on a nil by mouth regime, including no drinking of water, a tube was placed into my stomach to remove the build up of fluids until, as a last resort, it was decided to operate on Monday 16th. The operation was estimated to take 45 minutes to 2 hours, but lasted 4 hours due to what was discovered, with a further 30cm of my bowel being removed. In short my digestive system was blocked in a couple of places.

I have to admit that this was the lowest point of my whole journey which started on the 28th February 2008. I understand from those who saw me that I looked very unwell going into the operation, my body was extremely weak, so much so that a few days afterwards it took all my strength just to stand up and move to sit in my bedside chair.

I am now eating again, albeit small meals, and have been given additional food supplement drinks in order to built up my strength, but for now, it's good to be home and once again, I'm appreciating what I can do rather than what I can't do. Sadly I will not be fit enough to work at Spring Harvest this year and Ginny and I had hoped to have some time away next week, which we will now spend together at home.

Just prior to all this, I was sent the following words which on reflection seem so appropriate.

May the Lord show His mercy upon you:
May the light of His presence be your guide:
May He guard you and uphold you:
When you sleep, may His angels watch over you;
When you wake, may He fill you with His grace.
May you love Him and serve Him all your days,
Then in heaven may you see His face.

May the Lord's loving kindness surround you:
Keep you safe as you journey on your way:
May He lead you and inspire you
As He grants you the gift of each Day.

May He bless all your loved ones and cherish them:
Every friend, every stranger at your door:
In the name of His Son, our Saviour Christ, May God bless you,
now and evermore.

Current prayer requests are:
- ❖ I will regain my strength quickly.
- ❖ Healing of my wounds will progress well.
- ❖ Ginny and I will have a good week despite not going away.

Blessings
Graham

"But I will restore you to health and heal your wounds," declares the LORD. - Jeremiah 30 v 17

12 March 2009 – Book of Encouragement

24   The one who calls you is faithful and He will do it.

1 Thessalonians 5 v 24

(Email from Rev Chris Priddy – Son)

13 March 2009 – Prayer Newsletter 35

Well it's good to be home and thank you to everyone who has sent messages wishing Ginny and me an enjoyable week holidaying at home together. I have certainly appreciated some simple things of life which we so often take for granted, as - wait for it - I have enjoyed outings to Sainsbury's, the local garden centre, and Iceland. We have also had the opportunity of seeing a number of family members and friends, and I really appreciated getting to church last Sunday for the first time in seven weeks. However, it did bring home to me that I still have some way to go to regain my strength. Afternoon naps have become a feature of each day which then enables me to stay awake and watch evening TV.

Today I received this YouTube link from my eldest son Chris. Despite being almost 9 minutes long, do watch it and stick with it. The point at the end is so incredible, made us sit up and go wow http://www.youtube.com/watch?v=_e4zgJXPpI4.

It is five months today since the operation to remove the cancerous lump in my bowel and my rectum. Whilst that wound still requires daily attention I am reminded of an email last June from my nephew John quoting some words from Sir Winston Churchill in 1941.

Never, give in,
Never, never, never,
In nothing great or small,
Large or pretty,
Never give in except to the convictions of honour and good sense,
Never yield to the apparently overwhelming might of the enemy.

Between the age of 8 and 26, Boys Brigade played a big part of my life and its motto is 'Sure and Steadfast' taken from the verse in Hebrews 6 v 19 which says *'We have this hope (in Jesus) as an anchor for the soul, firm and secure (in Jesus).'* How true this is for those of us who are Christians.

This week I ask that you focus your prayers on a single request; that my open wounds will totally heal within the next 3 weeks.

Blessings
Graham

"But I will restore you to health and heal your wounds," declares the LORD. - Jeremiah 30 v 17

13 March 2009 – Book of Encouragement

What you shared with us on Wednesday at discipleship group was a huge shock, but thank you for allowing us to know the situation so we can pray more and more. Graham, your strong courage, faith and trust in God has been a huge encouragement to me. The many hymns and scripture verses you have previously sent have been so helpful.

It is so hard to know why God allows these situations, but what a comfort to know HE IS IN CONTROL.

I have a little book entitled God's little book of HOPE, and it has some really good references in it.

When a person prays, great things happen;

16 Therefore confess your sins to each other and pray
    for each other so that you may be healed.
    The prayer of a righteous man is powerful and effective.

James 5 v 16

In times of powerlessness it is comforting to know that God gives power to the weak, and to those who have might, He increases strength.

29 He gives strength to the weary
    and increases the power of the weak.

Isaiah 40 v 29

1   The Spirit of the Sovereign LORD is on me,
    because the LORD has anointed me
    to preach good news to the poor.
    He has sent me to bind up the broken-hearted,
    to proclaim freedom for the captives

Isaiah 61 v 1.

Remember, God is not bound by our circumstances, neither is He overcome by our turmoil. In every situation He has power to provide a way out for you. Put your hope in Him;

1   I lift up my eyes to the hills -
    where does my help come from?

2   My help comes from the LORD,
     the Maker of heaven and earth.
3   He will not let your foot slip -
     He who watches over you will not slumber;

Psalm 121 1-3

(Email from Mark and Ann Penson – Woodley Baptist Church)

13 March 2009 – Book of Encouragement

20   Now to Him who is able to do immeasurable
     more than we ask or imagine
     according to His power that is at working is.
21   to Him be glory in the church and in Christ
     Jesus throughout all generations,
     for ever and ever! Amen.

Ephesians 3 v 20-21

(Email from Audrey and Byron Goulding – Woodley Baptist Church)

19 March 2009 – Prayer Newsletter 36

Hi Everyone
This week I will start with a verse from Joshua 1 v 9; *'Have I not commanded you? Be strong and courageous. Do not be terrified; do not be discouraged, for the LORD your God will be with you wherever you go.'* As you read this prayer update, you will appreciate how appropriate this verse is to Ginny and me right now.

With these regular prayer letters I have invited so many people to follow my journey over the last year and as some of you have seen me around since returning home from hospital, this prayer letter is a little more difficult to write as its content will come as a shock to many of you who have faithfully supported Ginny & me in prayer.

While I was in hospital, it was discovered to the surprise of the whole medical team that the section of bowel removed during my last operation, when analysed was riddled with cancer cells despite all previous tests and scans showing that I had responded well to all treatments and the cancer had gone.

I have been advised that the cancer is now on the lining of my abdomen and therefore no further operations will be possible. Having said that, in a few weeks time, when I have rebuilt my strength and recovered from my last operation, I will commence a six month course of chemotherapy, being treated over a 48 hour period every two weeks. The aim of this is to contain the cancer and we have been advised that the six months following this course of chemotherapy will be critical.

The doctors have used the word 'contain the cancer', but in reality the chemotherapy treatment could provide one of the following outcomes.

1. It is ineffective and the cancer continues to grow and things get worse
2. It contains the cancer, meaning the cancer doesn't grow or shrink
3. It is totally effective and shrinks or kills the cancer cells

Forgive me for not sharing this in the last two updates, but I'm sure you will appreciate that it was important to us that we first spoke to our children and other family members, which we have now done.

Sadly, I believe it is now time for me to step down as Church Treasurer and I have spoken to David Barter and CLT about my decision which they acknowledge is right for me at this time.

At the outset of my cancer treatment, whilst at Spring Harvest, I gave my cancer to God to use for His good, whilst wanting to be healed. Despite this setback, the road ahead is very much in God's hands, but going forward we know that you and the fellowship at Woodley Baptist Church will continue to play a key part in supporting us.

As I conclude, my prayer is that your faith will not be shaken by this news and I will leave you with a verse sent to me by Hannah (a Spring Harvest steward) and taken from Nahum 1 v 7 *'The LORD is good, a stronghold in the day of trouble. He knows those who take refuge in Him'.*

Current prayer requests are;
- ❖ I will regain my strength quickly.
- ❖ Healing of my wounds will be completed prior to chemotherapy starting
- ❖ As a minimum, the cancer can be contained.

Blessings
Graham

"But I will restore you to health and heal your wounds," declares the LORD. - Jeremiah 30 v 17

Note: The above was sent to members and friends at Woodley Baptist Church. Slightly amended versions were sent to family and friends.

19 March 2009 – Book of Encouragement

10 So do not fear, for I am with you;
   do not be dismayed, for I am your God.
   I will strengthen you and help you;
   I will uphold you with my righteous right hand.

Isaiah 41 v 10

(Lucas on Life Bible Reading notes)

23 March 2009 – Book of Encouragement

8   I will instruct you and teach you in the way you should go;
   I will counsel you and watch over you.

Psalm 32 v 8

(Email from Jonathan Frater – Spring Harvest Steward)

27 March 2009 – Prayer Newsletter 37

First of all, I want to thank everyone who has supported us since I broke the news about my cancer having returned. Ginny and I have been deeply moved by your love, cards, emails, encouraging words and hugs, together with offers of practical help. We are so blessed to know each one of you. In fact I'm in tears as I write this and reflect on such friendships and the way God has brought us together.

The following song touched me so much at church on Sunday morning that I was unable to sing along as the words are so powerful in my current situation. Sadly it's not available on YouTube but I've managed to purchase a CD called Heritage and Hope by Chris Bowater. The first two verse and chorus is shown below,

> Greater Grace, deeper mercy,
> Wider love, higher ways.
> Perfect peace, complete forgiveness,
> It's all found in You,
> It's all found in You.
>
> It's all found in You, Jesus,
> It's all found in You.
> All I desire and all I require,
> It's all found in You.

© Chris Bowater, 1999 Sovereign Lifestyle Music

Last week I quoted a verse from Joshua 1 v 9; *'Have I not commanded you? Be strong and courageous. Do not be terrified; do not be discouraged, for the LORD your God will be with you wherever you go."* and this is becoming a key verse for me, having had it sent to me by a friend of Chris, and also by a team at the Department for Children, Schools and Families who my employer have a five year contract with.

Another relevant verse this week was in my daily Bible reading notes from Isaiah 41 v 10 *'So do not fear, for I am with you; do not be dismayed, for I am your God. I will strengthen you and help you; I will uphold you with my righteous right hand.'*

Reflecting back on the last week and a half, it's been both an enjoyable and an emotional period. Ginny and I managed a couple of days out together, visiting Windsor Castle and then the Ideal Home Show at Earls Court. However, despite taking opportunities to sit down every now and again, I realise now that it took its toll and took me three days to recover. At other times I have been dealing with some practical aspects of ensuring household paperwork is in joint names. Linked to this my church called a prayer meeting yesterday as a number of members are engaged in life and death issues, and being a part of that journey, it feels like a boat in a tumultuous sea, with the threat of being swamped by the next wave. As this was advertised, it brought home to me the seriousness of my illness.

However we can take encouragement from the following verses sent to me by Ann Penson.

James 5 v 16 *'When a person prays, great things happen'*

Isaiah 40 v 29 *'He gives strength to the weary and increases the power of the weak'*.

And I was reminded that God is not bound by our circumstances, neither is He overcome by our turmoil. In every situation He has power to provide a way out for you. Put your hope in Him.

John 14 v 13 & 14 says *'And I will do whatever you ask in my name, so that the Son may bring glory to the Father. You may ask me for anything in my name, and I will do it.'* In my Prayer update 35 I asked you to focus your prayers on a single request being that my open wounds will totally heal within the next 3 weeks. The excellent news is that the two open wounds from my last operation are now healed and don't require any dressings. The main wound from the October operation was really getting me down at the start of the week, as it had become messier and messier which required bulkier dressings which are very uncomfortable and has made sleeping difficult. However, this dramatically changed on Thursday and is significantly better, so much so that for the very first time my District Nurses will not be visiting me over the weekend and will review the situation on Monday. This again is excellent news and a real answer to my prayer. Thank you all and thank you Jesus but don't stop praying as this is such an important aspect of my recovery.

Current prayer requests are:
- ❖ I will continue to regain my strength
- ❖ Healing of my wound will be completed prior to chemotherapy starting
- ❖ I will be able to sleep better at nights
- ❖ As a minimum, the cancer will be contained.

Blessings
Graham

"But I will restore you to health and heal your wounds," declares the LORD. - Jeremiah 30 v 17

P.S. Please also pray for my father, whose brother died last night after a long illness, as well as for the rest of the family.

27 March 2009 – Book of Encouragement

9 I took you from the ends of the earth,
   from its farthest corners I called you.
   I said, 'You are my servant';
   I have chosen you and have not rejected you.
10 So do not fear, for I am with you;
   do not be dismayed, for I am your God.
   I will strengthen you and help you;
   I will uphold you with my righteous right hand.

Isaiah 41 v 9 - 10

(Email from Matt Partington – Woodley Baptist Church)

29 March 2009 – Book of Encouragement

8   I will lie down and sleep in peace,
for You alone, O LORD,
make me dwell in safety.

Psalm 4 v 8

Our church St Michael's in Aberystwth have been praying for you.

(Text from Daniel Priddy – Son)

29 March 2009 – Book of Encouragement

Dear Woodley Baptist Church Member
Many thanks for praying last Thursday evening for people within the fellowship facing major difficulties. In addition to the 25 people meeting at church, I know many of you were also praying wherever you were.

One of the clear outcomes of which I'm aware is regarding Graham Priddy. At 8 o'clock he was experiencing a lot of pain from the wound from his first operation; by 9 o'clock he was much more comfortable. Saturday morning was the first time for five and a half months that he didn't have a District Nurse attend him. He is delighted by this progress in healing, which has continued over the weekend. I'm sure he'll be updating you as usual later in the week, but I wanted to take opportunity to fuel your rejoicing and reinforce your expectation of God's power and grace.

Glory to God!

(Email from Pete Evens - Woodley Baptist Church Elder).

3 April 2009 – Prayer Newsletter 38

'The LORD is good, a refuge in times of trouble. He cares for those who trust in Him,'

Nahum 1 v 7

The LORD is good to those whose hope is in Him, to the one who seeks Him;

Lamentations 3 v 25

Praise the LORD, for the LORD is good; sing praise to His name, for He is gracious.

Psalm 135 v 3

Why have I stated with these verses, well it's been quite a week, let me explain.

Firstly, yesterday was the anniversary of my first operation and I thank God that He has brought me safely to this point, having supplied all my needs according to His riches during the past year.

Then last Thursday evening a prayer meeting was held at my church for people within the fellowship facing major difficulties. One of the clear outcomes was concerning my own situation. At 8 o'clock when the meeting started I texted to say I was experiencing a lot of pain from the wound from my October operation; by 9 o'clock I was much more comfortable.

Saturday morning, much to Ginny's delight, I enjoyed the first 'full' shower since 12 October, without having to worry about various wound dressings. This was also the first time for five and a half months that I didn't have a District Nurse visit to attend my wounds. In view of this I was able to attend the 9.00am Church Leadership Team meeting which previously I would have been unable to attend.

Sunday, Ginny and I travelled to Portsmouth to visit our son Richard who had moved house the day before. We arrived at his church just in time for the sermon which was all about healing the sick. It was a powerful sermon where I felt God saying, this is for you Graham, which made me feel a little uncomfortable. The final scripture verses were from Acts 5 v 15 & 16 which say *'As a result, people brought the sick into the streets and laid them on beds and mats so that at least Peter's shadow might fall on some of them as he passed by. Crowds gathered also from the towns around Jerusalem, bringing their sick and those tormented by evil spirits, and all of them were healed'.* Those last few words really hit home as the minister invited those who were sick to the walk to front of the church for prayer for healing. I have to say it took me a while to respond to God prompting, in a way it takes some guts to really trust what we read in the Bible, but I went to the front for prayer. I believe God did something in my life that day, but my illness is such that it's not visible and only medical tests will tell.

Monday, when my District Nurse visited again to check progress over the weekend it was agreed that no more daily visits would be necessary. However, they would ring occasionally to check that I'm OK. Whilst this is excellent news, I will miss the Nurses who have become friends over the last five and a half months.

This week I have also managed to walk to the local Post Office on a couple of occasions, again something that last week was too much to try and achieve.

Wednesday, I drove my car for the first time in two months and was able to drive to my Doctor's to collect my prescription. This trip was delayed by 24 hours as, when I tried on Tuesday, the battery was flat and the car wouldn't start.

This morning, I drove to the office to spend some time chatting with colleagues, who I miss, and I have to say I'm eagerly awaiting the day the Doctor will allow me back to work as I miss the challenge and the people contact this provides.

Since the start of the year I have asked people to pray that I will be totally recovered and 100% fit prior to Spring Harvest week 3 in Minehead. Following my last operation it became clear that I would no longer be able to attend this event to work with the stewarding team as in previous years, which was a massive disappointment to me. However, I think you all know me well enough by now to appreciate that I believe God hears our prayers and always answers even if it's not how we expect as in 1 John 5 v 14 -15 we read *'This is the confidence we have in approaching God: that if we ask anything according to His will, He hears us. And if we know that He hears us—whatever we ask—we know that we have what we asked of Him'.* Well, God has answered this prayer in an amazing way, as Ginny and I have been invited by Spring Harvest to attend as their guests so we will be travelling down to Minehead after Easter for the final week. It will be wonderful to see many friends who have supported me in prayer over the last year. Also this will be the first time we have managed to get away together since August Bank Holiday last year so we are both really looking forward to it, whilst appreciating the need to relax. It's also the only place I know where you can get gingerbread ice cream. To make the journey easier we are going to stop en route overnight with our dear friends in Sherborne.

Then last week I asked for prayer that I will be able to sleep better at nights and on Sunday night my youngest son Daniel texted me with the following verse from Psalm 4 v 8. *'I will lie down and sleep in peace, for You alone, O LORD make me dwell in safety'.* This was such an encouragement, and since then I have had some good nights, but on other occasions I still find it difficult to get comfortable enough to sleep well.

Finally, as most of this prayer letter is talking about answered prayer, periodically I have heard that churches with whom I have no connection are praying for me. If this is your church, could you please respond to this email, giving me the name of that church? (Those attending WBC need not respond ☺)

Current prayer requests are:
❖ I will continue to regain my strength
❖ Healing of my wound will be completed prior to chemotherapy starting
❖ I will be able to sleep better at nights
❖ As a minimum, the cancer will be contained.

May God Bless You Abundantly
Graham

"But I will restore you to health and heal your wounds," declares the LORD. - Jeremiah 30 v 17

4 April 2009 – Book of Encouragement

Following my last prayer update, I have established that the following churches with whom I have no personal contact are supporting me in prayer.

Church	Location
Ashford Common Baptist Church	Ashford
City Road Baptist Church and the Women's Fellowship	Winchester
Coalville	Leicestershire
Emmanuel Baptist Church	Hidiselu, Romania
Kings Church	Horsham
Pentre Jane Morgan Halls cell group	Aberystwyth University
St. Michaels	Aberystwyth
St. Nic's	Nottingham
St. Peters Church	Guildford
St. Catherine's (C of E) Church	Littleton, Prayer Support
Stretton Methodist Church Prayer Group & Church	Stretton, Shropshire
Upper Stratton Baptist Church	Upper Stratton
USBC and St Tom's	Sheffield
Vineyard cell group	St. Albans
Wesley Methodist Church	Weeke, Winchester
Woodley Baptist Church	Woodley
Wycliffe Baptist Church	Reading

4 April 2009 – Book of Encouragement

18 But the eyes of the Lord are on those who fear Him,
      on those whose hope is in His unfailing love,
      to deliver them from death and keep them alive in famine

Psalm 33:18

(Email from Roger and Pat Snelling - Friends in Sherborne)

Hi everyone,

People have often commented on how well I look and how positive I am concerning my illness. Whilst this is true, since my last operation when I was advised that the cancer had returned, I have spent time reflecting on the fact that I could die if the next phase of my treatment is unsuccessful and that I could be experiencing Spring Harvest or meeting some people or visiting places for the last time. This may surprise some of you but I write this so that you are aware that on occasions my emotions may not be what you expect and that these are thoughts I struggle with from time to time, especially as in heaven there will be no cancer.

A bookmark given to me the other week by Pam Mullin, a lady at my church who always smiles despite her own health issues, reads:

God has not promised skies ever blue,
Flower strewn pathways all through:
God has not promised sun without rain,
Joy without sorrow, peace without pain,

But He has promised strength for each day,
Rest after labour – light for our way.
Grace for all trials – help from above,
Unfailing sympathy, undying love.

Tomorrow is Good Friday, a day that makes us look at the cross where Jesus was left to hang in the intense heat with an unbearable thirst, exposed to the ridicule of the crowd, hanging in unthinkable pain for six hours while life slowly drained away until He died. These emotions remain real whilst knowing that it didn't end there as, three days later, we celebrate the fact that the tomb where He was laid was empty with no plausible explanation other than He had risen from the dead.

This week I came across this poem entitled 'What Easter Means to Me' which I can strongly relate to.

Easter morning, God be praised,
Jesus Christ from death was raised.

On Good Friday, Jesus died;
All for us, He was crucified.

Jesus bore the pain for me,
From my sin, to set me free.

Death could not confine our Lord,
And to life He was restored.

Easter morn we consecrate,
His resurrection to celebrate.

Jesus' love means when we die,
We'll live in heaven with Him on high.

Our Saviour loves us awesomely;
That's what Easter means to me.
Hallelujah.

Author unknown

When I visited my office last week my director made the observation that I was the sort of person used to giving of myself and supporting others, rather than receiving help. He is so right and it's not easy, but I am starting to learn to accept help when offered rather than just saying it's OK even when I know that I can't do it.

This week I have been so blessed by Dave who cut my grass on Saturday morning and my discipleship group who painted my kitchen ceiling when they met at our house on Wednesday evening. I didn't share this with Dave but whilst he was cutting my grass, I was reading my Lent Bible study and came across Hebrews 10 v 24 *'And let us show concern for each other, doing what we can to display love and show kindness'*. & 13 v 16 *'Never forget to do good or to help one another, for it is sacrifices such as these that are pleasing to God'*.

Yesterday I saw my Oncologist to discuss my next phase of treatment which should begin within the next three weeks after I have had another CT scan which will be used as a baseline going forward. My treatment will involve a small operation to have a Peripherally Inserted Central Catheter (PICC line) fitted, so that two chemotherapy drugs, Oxaliplatin and 5FU (Fluorouracil), can be fed into my body, plus anti-sickness drugs and a vitamin called folinic acid which makes the 5FU more effective.

So once a fortnight on a Tuesday I will first be given the Oxaliplatin along with the folinic acid over a two hour period, following which the 5FU will be given to me over a 46 hour period via a small portable pump which avoids the need for an overnight stay. This will then be disconnected on a Thursday by my District Nurse. As before, there is a long list of possible side effects but I have been told to expect numbness or tingling in my hands and feet and that anything cold should be avoided (so extra cold Guinness will be off the menu this hot summer). I also learnt that, other than the power of prayer, it is unlikely the chemotherapy will totally kill off all the cancer cells as the aim is to contain the cancer, meaning the cancer doesn't grow or shrink.

During my appointment with the Oncologist, he prescribed some antibiotics for the wound on my bottom as this is still causing some issues.

In Prayer Newsletter 11 on 20th June I included a famous song that had encouraged me called Amazing Grace. This week I'm going to include another version which again encourages me so much as I appreciate God's goodness to me and the Hope He promises as once we have asked God to release those chains of sin, then He is forever mine. I first came across this song at the Mandate conference I attended in November 2007 where 4000 men sang it at a time when my symptoms were just beginning to get me down. The YouTube link is http://www.youtube.com/watch?v=MXl9nWLsJtk&feature=related and the accompanying graphics are an excellent reminder of the pain Jesus suffered on the cross and then the promise of His unending love, with such amazing grace.

Amazing grace how sweet the sound
That saved a wretch like me!

I once was lost, but now I'm found
Was blind, but now I see.

'Twas grace that taught my heart to fear
And grace my fears relieved;
How precious did that grace appear
The hour I first believed.

My chains are gone
I've been set free
My God, my Saviour has ransomed me.
And like a flood His mercy reigns
Unending love, amazing grace.

The Lord has promised good to me,
His word my hope secures;
He will my shield and portion be
As long as life endures.

My chains are gone
I've been set free
My God, my Saviour has ransomed me.
And like a flood His mercy reigns
Unending love, amazing grace.

The earth shall soon dissolve like snow
The sun forbear to shine.
But God, who called me here below
Will be forever mine
Will be forever mine
You are forever mine.

© Chris Tomlin, Worshiptogether.com Songs; Six Steps Music

This will be my last prayer letter until I return from Spring Harvest and I pray that you will experience afresh the true meaning of Easter and enjoy yourselves, whatever plans you may have. So to conclude - Easter is a wonderful celebration of life and you may wish to celebrate by listening to the following YouTube clip which, whilst not in the Big Top at Spring Harvest, has similar worship.

http://www.youtube.com/watch?v=UWndDW_271g

Current prayer requests are;

- ❖ Ginny & I will have a wonderful break at Spring Harvest, do enough but not overdo things.
- ❖ I will continue to regain my strength
- ❖ The antibiotics will speed up the healing of my wound
- ❖ I will be able to sleep better at nights as this is still a problem
- ❖ The cancer will not grow prior to chemotherapy starting

May God Bless You Abundantly
Graham

"But I will restore you to health and heal your wounds," declares the LORD. - Jeremiah 30 v 17

So what is a PICC line?

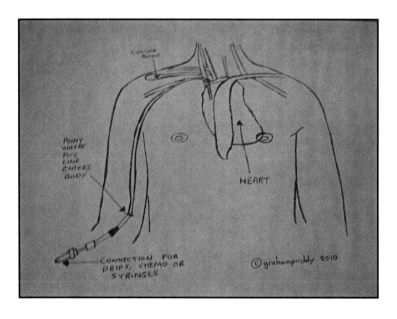

A PICC line is a more recent development to the Hickman line which I had in May 2008. It is a thin flexible silicone tube which is inserted into one of the large veins in the arm (usually near the bend of the elbow) from where it is threaded into the superior vena cava. The initials PICC stand for peripherally inserted central catheter.

PICC lines are normally inserted as an outpatient. Some local anaesthetic cream is applied to the skin which usually ensures the insertion is painless. The procedure takes about 30 to 40 minutes. Once the PICC line is in place it will be taped firmly to the skin with a special transparent dressing to stop it coming out of the vein. A chest x-ray will then be taken to check the position of the line before it is used.

The PICC line can be used for taking blood for blood tests, giving chemotherapy drugs or giving blood transfusions.

9 April 2009 – Book of Encouragement

Simply trusting every day
Trusting through the stormy way
Even when my faith is small,
Trusting Jesus, that is all.

Brightly doth His spirit shine
Into this poor heart of mine,
While He leads I cannot fall,
Trusting Jesus, that is all.

Singing if my way be clear,
Praying if the path is drear,
If in danger, for Him call,
Trusting Jesus, that is all.

Trusting as the moments fly
Trusting as the days go by,
Trusting Him what'er befall,
Trusting Jesus, that is all.

Author Edgar P. Stites, 1876.

1   "Trust in God; trust also in Me."

John 14 v 1

(Email from Mark and Ann Penson – Woodley Baptist Church)

9 April 2009 – Book of Encouragement

The following is an amazing song which has over 9,600,000 views on YouTube so I would encourage you to check out the following YouTube link and enjoy 5 minutes of pure encouragement and inspiration http://www.youtube.com/watch?v=CT7x3VnrqbA Sadly in this book I can only quote the first verse but do check out the YouTube link.

Who I am?
That the Lord of all the earth,
Would care to know my name,
Would care to feel my hurt.
Who am I?
That the bright and morning star,
Would choose to light the way,
For my ever wandering heart.
© Casting Crowns (Davis/Collins/Gray/Thompson/Harding/Smart/Saunders), Sony/ATV Music Publishing LLC, Warner/Chappell Music, Inc - Reunion Records

(Email from Matt Partington – Woodley Baptist Church)

11 April 2009 – Book of Encouragement

22 Cast your cares on the Lord
     and He will sustain you;
     He will never let the righteous fall.

Psalm 55 v 22

(Email from Rev David Priddy – Brother)

20 April 2009 - Book of Encouragement

I read the attached in my 555 time1 yesterday morning after praying for you and want to encourage you to hold fast to God's promise to be with you no matter what. The words of Isaiah 40 v 28 to end had also come to mind whilst praying, that your strength will be renewed for your treatment to come so that your body will be prepared and ready. May you and Ginny know God's peace and strength today. Isaiah 40 v 28 reads *'Do you not know? Have you not heard? The LORD is the everlasting God, the Creator of the ends of the earth. He will not grow tired or weary, and His understanding no one can fathom'*. Much blessing, Dot.

Focus on God's Promises

13 For I am the LORD, your God,
    who takes hold of your right hand and says to you,
    Do not fear; I will help you.

Isaiah 41 v 13

The Lord says to you this morning the same thing He told Jacob in a dream:

"I am with you and will watch you (i.e keep watch over you with care, take notice of you) wherever you may go, and I will bring you back to this land; for I will not leave you" (Genesis 28 v 15). Keep your mind on this promise in spite of any news you may hear that tempts you to be afraid today.

God promises to be with you, watch over you with care, take notice of you wherever you may go, and bring you back again. He says He will not leave you, and He will complete all that He promises He has made for you. This means that no weapon formed against you will prosper. (See Isaiah 54 v 17)

---

1 555 time means praying 5 minutes in the morning, lunchtime and evening.

(Email from Dot Butler – Woodley Baptist Church

Note: This was sent on the 17 March 2009 but arrived 20 April which was when I really needed it and we believe the internet delay was down to God's perfect timing.

23 April 2009 – Book of Encouragement

3   ....I will give you the treasures of darkness,
      and hidden wealth of secret places......

Isaiah 45:3

(Email from David Stillman – Woodley Baptist Church Elder)

24 April 2009 – Prayer Newsletter 40

Hi everyone,

Ginny and I had a lovely break away with our friends in Sherborne and then at Spring Harvest, although Spring Harvest was very different to the previous nine years that I have been going. The head office staff have been praying regularly for me during the year and maybe as a joke I was given a volunteer team badge saying I was a 'Special Guest', so any chance of being humble quickly disappeared. During the week I discovered a number of things.

Medically I was unable to sit for the duration of the evening celebrations or teaching seminars. However, as Big Top events are televised, when it got too much for me I was able to return to my chalet for the ending.

Personally it was good meeting up with so many friends who have been supporting me in prayer and I discovered that certain friendships were far deeper than I had appreciated. God also puts you in touch with the right people at the right time, even if it was just carrying our cases from the car to our chalet. Sadly Butlins have closed the ice cream stand that sold gingerbread ice cream.

Spiritually, I was very keen to spend a few hours, as I had the year before, in the prayer room as this had been of such value. However, this year it was a total downer and I was wrong to expect God to respond in a similar way to the year before, which is a lesson in itself. In my personal reflections I believe God is saying to me that He will heal me, but I need to wait until He is ready. Currently I keep being brought back to these verses in Isaiah 40 v 28 – 31; *28 'Do you not know? Have you not heard? The LORD is the everlasting God, the Creator of the ends of the earth. He will not grow tired or weary, and His understanding no one can fathom. 29 He gives strength to the weary and increases the power of the weak. 30 Even youths grow tired and weary, and young men stumble and fall; 31 but those who hope in the LORD will renew their strength.* They will soar on wings like eagles; they will run and not grow weary, they will walk and not be faint.

Looking back on the week, the two highlights were meeting up with Ishmael and his wife Irene for an hour and a half, sharing our individual experiences of God's goodness and faithfulness in our individual struggles against cancer. For those who don't know Ishmael (like my Dad) Ishmael is a well known songwriter, author and Christian communicator. He has a unique global ministry among children and has a real heart for seeing all ages praising God and having fun together. The second was after I had to leave the Big Top Celebration Communion Celebration, due to being uncomfortable, and returned to my chalet to continue watching it on TV and spending time on my knees before God and sharing communion using some bread and grape juice I found.

Whilst I was at Spring Harvest I bought a CD called Rites of Passage by Paul Field and Dan Wheeler who performed it there. This song called Rest in Me has struck me every time I have listened to it.

The song is called Some days the world seems but I will just quote the chorus and last verse which provides the encouragement that:-

You can rest in Me when you're weary
you can rest in Me through the tears
in My eyes you'll see
a glimpse of eternity
so you can rest in Me.
I can't take all your pain away this side of heaven's door
but I can be a comfort when you're hurting
in all your uncertainty My love for you is sure

149

you are beautiful
and you are blessed
You can rest in Me

© Paul Field/Dan Wheeler

This song encourages me as, to be honest, I have been in constant pain since returning home, so much so that I asked the District Nurse to visit a day earlier than planned and it has effectively stopped me doing anything. I think that my bum wound has become damaged and she is discussing this with the rest of the team to know how to treat this. The pain has kept me awake for long periods each evening and I have been on my knees crying out to God to take the pain away with the need to nap during the day. Hence the words of the song above become relevant just now.

It never ceases to amaze me how God uses other people to bless and encourage me with just the right words when the going gets tough as it did on Monday when Dot Butler sent me the following entitled 'Focus on God's Promises'.

13 For I am the LORD, your God,
   who takes hold of your right hand and says to you,
   Do not fear; I will help you.

Isaiah 41 v 13

The Lord says to you this morning the same thing He told Jacob in a dream: *"I am with you and will (keep over you with care, take notice of) you wherever you may go, and I will bring you back to this land; for I will not leave you"* (Genesis 28 v 15). Keep your mind on this promise in spite of any news you may hear that tempts you to be afraid today.

God promises to be with you, watch over you with care, take notice of you wherever you may go, and bring you back again, He says He will not leave you, and He will complete all that He promises He has made for you. This means that no weapon formed against you will prosper. (see Isaiah 54 v 17).

My son Daniel, along with a few others, have suggested I use these prayer letters as a basis for a book which, after much thought, I have started to write. However, this does seem a massive challenge with the need to ensure copyright is obtained for the various songs I have included and how to obtain a publisher's interest.

The good news is that I return to the hospital this morning for a CT scan, in preparation for my operation on Monday at 9.00am to fit my PICC line. My chemotherapy will start on Tuesday at 10.00am when I will first be given the Oxaliplatin and the folinic acid over a two hour period, following which the 5FU will be given to me over a 46 hour period via a small portable pump which my District Nurse will disconnect on Thursday. Knowing the hospital system well now, I am expecting to spend most of the day at the hospital on Tuesday.

Current prayer requests are:
❖ The wound will heal and the pain and discomfort will go
❖ I will be able to sleep better at nights as this is still a problem
❖ That the treatment will be 100% effective
❖ The PICC line will be inserted without problems
❖ The side effects from the chemotherapy will be minimal and bearable
❖ The chemotherapy will be 100% effective

May God Bless You Abundantly
Graham

"But I will restore you to health and heal your wounds," declares the LORD. - Jeremiah 30 v 17

22 April 2009 - Book of Encouragement

17 no weapon forged against you will prevail,
   and you will refute every tongue that accuses you.
   This is the heritage of the servants of the LORD,
   and this is their vindication from me,"
   declares the LORD.

Isaiah 54 v 17

(Text from Rev David Priddy – Brother)

22 April 2009 - Book of Encouragement

Praying. You must be very tired of it all. May the Peace of Jesus flood your soul and may His name bring healing to your wounds. Strength in the Name of Jesus. Hope in His name. Peace in the name of Jesus. Rest in His name. Jesus, Jesus, Jesus. x x

(Text from Lucy Tovey – Spring Harvest Chief Steward)

23 April 2009 - Book of Encouragement

Sound good all in all, will pray that the antibiotics work well. Good pain being relieved. At discipleship group last night it was really obvious that we were all sharing in this with you and Ginny in a very heartfelt way. Lots of ardent prayer! Dave has just been reading about the Red Sea. It looked such an obstacle BUT GOD brought them through in a fantastic way. Read Moses' song of peace in Exodus 15 which includes praise for victories ahead.

(Text from Ann Redfern – Woodley Baptist Church)

6   His left arm is under my head,
    and his right arm embraces me.

Song of Solomon 2 v 6

27 The eternal God is your refuge,
    and underneath are the everlasting arms.
    He will drive out your enemy before you,
    saying, 'Destroy him!'

Deuteronomy 33 v 37

30 But when he saw the wind, he was afraid and,
    beginning to sink, cried out, "Lord, save me!"
31 Immediately Jesus reached out His hand and caught him.
    "You of little faith," He said, "why did you doubt?"

Matthew 14 v 30-31

23 If the LORD delights in a man's way,
    He makes his steps firm;
24 though he stumble, he will not fall,
    for the LORD upholds him with His hand.

Psalm 37 v 23-24

12 About Benjamin He said:
    "Let the beloved of the LORD rest secure in Him,
    for He shields him all day long,
    and the one the LORD loves rests between His shoulders."

Deuteronomy 33 v 12

2   Be shepherds of God's flock that is under your care,
    serving as overseers—not because you must,
    but because you are willing,

as God wants you to be; not greedy for money,
but eager to serve;

1 Peter 5 v 2

8   For this is what the LORD Almighty says: "After
he has honoured me and has sent me against
the nations that have plundered you—for whoever
touches you touches the apple of His eye.

Zechariah 2 v 8

28 I give them eternal life, and they shall never perish;
no one can snatch them out of my hand.
29 My Father, who has given them to me, is greater than all;
no one can snatch them out of my Father's hand

John 10 v 28-29

(Text from Ann Redfern – Woodley Baptist Church)

26 April 2009 - Book of Encouragement

15 For this reason, ever since I heard about your faith in the Lord
Jesus and your love for all the saints,
16 I have not stopped giving thanks for you,
remembering you in my prayers.
17 I keep asking that the God of our Lord
Jesus Christ, the glorious
Father, may give you the Spirit of wisdom and revelation,
so that you may know Him better.
18 I pray also that the eyes of your heart
may be enlightened in order
that you may know the hope to which He has called you,
the riches of His glorious inheritance in the saints,
19 and His incomparably great power for us who believe.
That power is like the working of His mighty strength,

20 Which He exerted in Christ when He
    raised Him from the dead and
    seated Him at His right hand in the heavenly realms,

Ephesians 1 v 15 - 20

(Text from Mary Hearn – Sister-in-Law)

1 May 2009 – Prayer Newsletter 41

Hi everyone,

Sorry for the length of this week's prayer update but a lot has happened in the last week and a half. My last prayer letter was in draft format when I issued it in a rush while Ginny was packing my bag for an emergency admission into hospital on Wednesday evening of 22 April, after having visited my doctor due to being in constant pain for three days and having a temperature of 38°. It was an unpleasant admission as on arrival there were no free beds and trying to sit in the waiting room was sheer agony in view of the fact that I couldn't sit. At times I ended up kneeling on the floor with my head on the chair.

Once seen by the surgical doctor, the reason I was in so much pain became apparent. My wound from my first operation had grown some additional skin called hypergranulation tissue which was also the cause of my wound becoming so messy in recent weeks. This was treated with a mixture of three different antibiotics and acid to eat the additional tissue growth.

While in hospital the planned CT scan took place and has shown that, whilst my kidneys and liver remain free from cancer, there was evidence of cancer tissue around the area of my original operation; hence I am keen to get the chemotherapy started.

Monday turned out to be an emotional day as, when I went to have my PICC line inserted at 9.00am following which I was to be discharged, I was advised that they were unhappy to go ahead without my Oncologist's confirmation in view of the treatment that I was receiving for the hypergranulation tissue, the antibiotics I was on and the condition of my wound. Unfortunately my Oncologist had the day off and I was subsequently booked in to see him at 9.20am before his clinic started on Tuesday. I therefore decided to stay in hospital for a further night which turned out to be a real blessing. More about this later.

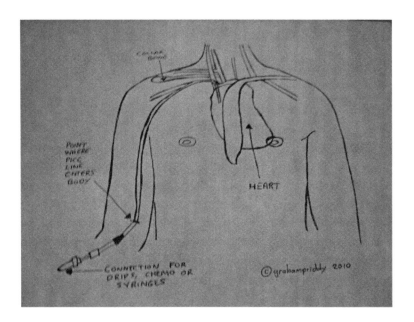

Tuesday was another emotional day as, at the outset of my consultation, my Oncologist said he wasn't prepared to allow the chemotherapy to go ahead as my wound hadn't totally healed. I asked whether he had seen the results of my CT scan - which he hadn't. He reviewed the results and then agreed to allow chemotherapy to go ahead on the basis that the wound is closely monitored as the chemotherapy drugs could have an adverse affect on the healing process.

I then went and had the PICC line inserted followed by an X-ray to check that the line had been correctly sited near my heart. However, the X-ray showed that the catheter had followed a vein up into my neck instead. This meant that the whole procedure had to be repeated with the second X-ray showing all was well. By this time it was almost 3.00pm and too late to start my chemotherapy so it was agreed I that I would return on Wednesday morning when they would see me as soon as I arrived. During the procedure I was reminded of Psalm 139 v 14 'I Praise You Lord, for I am astonishingly and awesomely made; Your works are truly wonderful; My Soul knows it full well.' Bear in mind that it will be my heart that pumps the 46 hour drug through the PICC line.

Wednesday's chemotherapy session went well and I left the hospital at 2.00pm, having spent an enjoyable time lying on a bed, drinking tea, listening to my iPod and reading my book entitled 'The End of Life's Journey' about sharing Christ's victory over death and offering compassion to those who have lost loved ones. Before leaving I was connected up to the 5FU drug for the next 46 hours, given a large medical bucket for when the District Nurse disconnects it on Friday, plus a variety of medication, some to be taken at breakfast and lunch, others in the evening plus some more just in case. These are in addition to the variety of drugs I am already taking for pain relief. This means I take a mixture of eight pills, three times a day. Finally I was told that if my temperature rises to 38 degrees, or if I get uncontrollable shakes, to go immediately to the A & E department, explaining that I need to be seen urgently. Being on chemotherapy again means I need to be extra careful to stay away from others with colds and infections as these could have a serious impact on my own health, so please bear this in mind when approaching me.

Back to Monday evening: despite the disappointment about the PICC line being delayed, even with my normal pain relief, I was in a lot of pain due to problems with my waterworks which was only put in check with morphine. At lunchtime, I received a phone call from a good friend Denice Lowen asking whether some members of the Bill Johnston healing ministry team who were in Reading could come to the ward and pray for my healing. I agreed, cleared it with the ward sister and spent an emotional afternoon reflecting on God's word about healing and trying to work out if I was in the right frame of mind for when the team arrived. This was helped by an unexpected visit by my minister, David Barter, who acknowledged that I should just do it. The team of five arrived at 6.30pm, we drew the curtains around my bed and after a few introductions, I was advised not to pray with them, but just to receive God's healing as they prayed for the Holy Spirit to come and heal me. It's hard to describe the next half hour other than to say that the problems I had been experiencing with my waterworks all week have been resolved and any healing of my cancer may take longer to experience but I am still trusting God's word, His Holy Spirit and

Jesus to act. I can however report that since these prayers my wound is significantly cleaner. I have shared this with my Surgeon on Thursday afternoon as I believe God's healing works alongside the medical profession, which she warmly acknowledged.

I have been overwhelmed with your love this week - John Russell from my discipleship group cut my grass and one portion of scripture sent to me by my sister-in-law Mary Hearn is from my favourite chapter of the Bible. Ephesians 1 encouraged me greatly while I was in hospital. From verse 15 we read *'15 For this reason, ever since I heard about your faith in the Lord Jesus and your love for all the saints, 16 I have not stopped giving thanks for you, remembering you in my prayers. 17 I keep asking that the God of our Lord Jesus Christ, the glorious Father, may give you the Spirit of wisdom and revelation, so that you may know Him better. 18 I pray also that the eyes of your heart may be enlightened in order that you may know the hope to which He has called you, the riches of His glorious inheritance in the saints, 19 and His incomparably great power for us who believe. That power is like the working of His mighty strength, 20 Which He exerted in Christ when He raised Him from the dead and seated Him at His right hand in the heavenly realms,*

What encouraged me was that it relates to others interceding for me at this time and that I normally focus on verses 1-14 which to me says it all, but I will leave you to look it up or read it in my prayer letter number 10 if you still have it.

And a poem called Precious Child by Avril Hoper sent to me by Pat Snelling who I stayed with recently. The poem is based on Isaiah 43 v 1 *'But now, this is what the LORD says - He who created you, O Jacob, He who formed you, O Israel: "Fear not, for I have redeemed you; I have summoned you by name; you are mine'.*

I Love you Child
You're mine, You're mine
One day you will know
My Love Divine.

Keep pressing on
I have heard your prayer
I know your heart

I know your care.

True joy will come
As you listen to me
I have given you my word
My holy Key.

It will lead you on
To pastures new
And open up
Great treasures for you.

Please keep on trusting
Have faith to the end,
I need your love
You are my friend.

Lord Jesus.

© Avril Hoper

Tonight my discipleship group have organised a surprise meal out which is a lovely way to end a difficult and emotional two weeks.

Next appointments

Monday
- morning District Nurse visits for blood tests

Tuesday
- 10:10am Clinic appointment with Oncologist at Berkshire Cancer Unit
- 10:30am Chemotherapy treatment
- 15:30pm Outpatients clinic with Mr Farouk, Registrar

Thursday
- afternoon District Nurse disconnects chemotherapy pump

Current prayer requests are:
- ❖ The wound will heal without further delay and the discomfort will go
- ❖ I will be able to sleep better at nights as this is still a problem
- ❖ The side effects from the chemotherapy will be minimal and bearable
- ❖ My stoma will not be affected by the chemotherapy drugs and pills
- ❖ The chemotherapy will be 100% effective
- ❖ I will not catch any infections

To conclude, in my last update I explained that 'It never ceases to amaze me how God uses other people to bless and encourage me with just the right words when the going gets tough as it did on Monday when Dot Butler sent me the following entitled 'Focus on God's Promises' quoting from Isaiah 41 v 13. *'For I am the LORD, your God, who takes hold of your right hand and says to you, do not fear; I will help you'.*

What I didn't know at the time was that Dot had actually emailed this to me on 17th March but it didn't arrive in my inbox until Monday 20th April when I really needed to read it. Dot and I both believe that God obviously had a reason for holding it back until I really needed it. Isn't He great!!

May God Bless You Abundantly
Graham

"But I will restore you to health and heal your wounds," declares the LORD. - Jeremiah 30 v 17

3 May 2009 - Book of Encouragement

May I run the race before me,
strong and brave to face the foe,
looking only unto Jesus,
as I onward go.

(Email from Norman Priddy – Dad)

3 May 2009 - Book of Encouragement

Our God is an awesome God, He is Sovereign and all Powerful, He is Omnipotent, Omnipresent, He is Compassionate and Loving. He is Holy and Faithful and never fails those who love Him. He is the Alpha and Omega, the Author and Perfector of our faith, and yet He cares for us all and delights in us.

Wishing you every blessing, and prayer, knowing that His will is your desire.

(Facebook note from John Hillman – Spring Harvest Chief Steward)

8 May 2009 – Prayer Newsletter 42

Greeting everyone,

First of all, I have been invited to attend as a VIP cancer survivor at an event called Relay for Life to be held on 20th-21st June 2009 at Reading Rugby Club on behalf of Cancer Research UK.

Cancer Research UK is the world's leading independent organisation dedicated to cancer research. They support research into all aspects of cancer through the work of more than 4,250 scientists, doctors and nurses. Over the past ten years alone, thousands of lives have been saved through earlier detection and improved treatments. But, much work remains to be done if we are to achieve our aim of beating cancer.

If you would like to assist my fund raising efforts and meeting my £1,000 target, you may do so on-line at

http://www.donatetomyrelay.org/grahampriddyoronmyFacebookpage at http://www.facebook.com/profile.php?id=602116630&ref=profile. If you are a UK tax payer, donations can be gift aided on-line. Currently I have raised £130.00

I'm not sure about being able to find people mad enough to create a 24 hour relay team, but if you are up for it, let me know, further details are shown here http://www.cancerresearchuk.org/relay/venues/reading/ Do look up the link, as the Candle of Hope celebration at dusk is another highlight of the event.

On reflection, I think this may have been the toughest week outside of the hospital environment so far, but with this come joyful moments. We had a wonderful evening last Friday with my discipleship group who organised a surprise meal out. As I walked in 45 minutes late, greeted by so many smiles, it sunk in how special this group of people are to me, knowing that they feel my ups and downs, share my tears and smiles and are very much in this fight with me. Bank Holiday Monday was lovely too when our parents came for lunch and the afternoon, even though they could see I was struggling. Sadly I was too exhausted to watch Ginny, her father & brother enjoy their long awaited hot air balloon flight on Saturday.

I have been put in touch with a Macmillan Nurse who is due to visit me at home to assess whether additional support, help or medication may make my life more comfortable at this stage of my treatment.

I have always been honest in these updates, which at times isn't easy. However, so that you understand, since coming off chemotherapy and various pills on Friday afternoon, I have felt washed out, been sick, had diarrhoea and not slept well which has meant I haven't really done anything other than go and watch Reading play on Saturday afternoon, which resulted in me going straight to bed when I got home. To be frank, it's not been fun just now.

However, I think you will appreciate by now how much I value and believe in the power of prayer so on Monday evening I sent a text to two people I respect dearly asking that they would commit to praying nightly for me. My text read, 'I don't like bedtime, don't sleep well, nights long, they scare me a bit, despite trusting Jesus'.

One reply said, 'No problem, it will be my privilege. It's OK to be scared as Jesus knows exactly how you feel – Gethsemane. He won't let go of you or condemn you'. The other said 'we have a huge God bigger than our fears; He has your name written on the palm of your hands'. Needless to say, once I settled down I had my first comfortable night for months. ☺

On Tuesday my Bible reading notes focused on Luke 12 v 22 – 26 which reads *22 Then Jesus said to His disciples: "Therefore I tell you,* do not worry about your life, *what you will eat; or about your body, what you will wear. 23 Life is more than food, and the body more than clothes. 24 Consider the ravens: They do not sow or reap, they have no storeroom or barn; yet God feeds them.* And how much more valuable you are than birds! *25 Who of you by worrying can add a single hour to his life? 26 Since you cannot do this very little thing, why do you worry about the rest?* ☺

Our friends Mark and Linda Hallett sent me the following a little while back which feels appropriate just now

Hide me now under Your wings.
Cover me within Your mighty hand.

Chorus.
When the oceans rise and thunders roar,
I will soar with You above the storm.
Father, You are King over the flood;
I will be still and know You are God.

Find rest, my soul, in Christ alone.
Know His power in quietness and trust.

Repeat chorus

© Reuben Morgan

Wednesday morning I woke thinking of Psalm 103 v 1 – 3 *'1 Praise the LORD, O my soul; all my inmost being, praise His holy name. 2 Praise the LORD, O my soul, and forget not all His benefits – 3 who forgives all your sins and heals all your diseases',* as for the first time since last Friday, I felt ready to start the day. Since then I have been generally OK, but struggle slightly by early evening.

Next appointments

Monday
- ❖ morning District Nurse visits for Blood tests
- ❖ Afternoon Macmillan Nurse visits

Tuesday
- ❖ 10:10am Clinic appointment with Oncologist at Berkshire Cancer Unit
- ❖ 10:30am Chemotherapy treatment
- ❖ 15:30pm Outpatients clinic with Mr Farouk, Registrar

Thursday
- ❖ afternoon District Nurse disconnects chemotherapy pump

Current prayer requests are;
- ❖ The wound will heal without further delay and the discomfort will go
- ❖ I will be able to sleep better at nights as this is still a problem
- ❖ My next chemotherapy will go well with side effects being minimal and bearable
- ❖ My stoma will not be affected by the chemotherapy drugs and pills
- ❖ The chemotherapy will be 100% effective
- ❖ I will not catch any infections

May God Bless You Abundantly
Graham

"But I will restore you to health and heal your wounds," declares the LORD. - Jeremiah 30 v 17

15 May 2009 – Prayer Newsletter 43

Greetings everyone,

Many thanks to those of you who have already responded to my fund raising at an event called Relay for Life to be held on 20th-21st June 2009 at Reading Rugby Club on behalf of Cancer Research UK.

Currently I have raised

- ❖ £190.00 towards my £1000.00 target.
- ❖ 4 people from work have agreed to be part of my team
- ❖ 2 people from church have agreed to be part of my team
- ❖ 4 Spring Harvest Stewards have shown an interest in coming down to support me.

If you are still thinking of sponsoring the links are http://www.donatetomyrelay.org/grahampriddy or on my Facebook page at http://www.facebook.com/profile.php?id=602116630&ref=profile. Or let me know if you are mad enough to join these already supporting me on the day.

Further details are shown here http://www.cancerresearchuk.org/relay/venues/reading/

After the effects of my first chemotherapy session I have decided to keep these weeks as relaxing as possible until I fully understand the effect on my body. Tuesday's session went well and means I'm at the hospital between 4.5 to 5 hours. However, the time went quickly with a combination of Bible study, reading a book on healing, listening to music, playing battleships and chatting with fellow patients.

I had a very encouraging one and a half hour chat with a Macmillan Nurse on Monday afternoon who is now arranging for a home visit from an Occupation Therapist, some home aromatherapy or massage and some sleeping pills via my doctor to assist my pain relief management. During this visit, as we explored my whole treatment since visiting my doctor in December 2007, it was clear that I have been through a lot, more than most people with bowel cancer. However, on a personal front, God has clearly been changing me as a person (for the better I would add, ☺) and been using my cancer to encourage others as was my original prayer. This reminded me of some words given by Bill Smith, a Spring Harvest steward at Skegness in 2008, days before my first operation which were *being confident of this, that He who began a good work in you will carry it on to completion until the day of Christ Jesus'* from Philippians 1 v 6. How true this has been.

My week has been generally good, sleeping slightly better (without sleeping pills mentioned above) and my wound seems to be less weepy, which has cheered me up no end. Current side effects to the chemotherapy seem to be a slight loss of taste and tingling fingertips at times when holding items that are cold, which make certain things rather difficult at time. I also experience the occasional feeling of sickness.

Last Sunday at church we sang a really old hymn which has amazing words and to my surprise I also found a beautifully sung version on YouTube, link being http://www.youtube.com/watch?v=Ew3yXqdMF1o However, it does omit verse 2.

1. My hope is built on nothing less
    than Jesus' blood and righteousness.
    I dare not trust the sweetest frame,
    but wholly lean on Jesus' name.

Refrain:
    On Christ the solid rock I stand,
    all other ground is sinking sand;
    all other ground is sinking sand.

2. When Darkness seems to hide his face,
    I rest on His unchanging grace.
    In every high and stormy gale,
    my anchor holds within the veil.

(Refrain)

3. His oath, His covenant, His blood
    supports me in the whelming flood.
    When all around my soul gives way,

He then is all my hope and stay.

(Refrain)

4. When He shall come with trumpet sound,
    O may I then in Him be found!
    Dressed in His righteousness alone,
    faultless to stand before the throne!

(Refrain)

© Edward Mote 1834 Public Domain

Next Wednesday, Ginny and I are off to Swanage until Sunday, staying at a house overlooking the sea that has been kindly donated to us, which coincides with Ginny's 'Special' birthday. We are praying that this will be an enjoyable, relaxing break, being able to see a few places without overdoing things. We are so blessed to have such wonderful, caring friends, who never cease to amaze me with their generosity; kindness, odd cooked meal and time. My discipleship group have now created a weekly rota for cutting my lawn which I am unable to manage at present.

Next week's appointments

Monday
✧   morning District Nurse visits for Blood tests

Current prayer requests are:
✧   The wound will heal without further delay and the discomfort will go
✧   I will be able to sleep better at nights as this is still a problem
✧   My next chemotherapy will go well with side effects being minimal and bearable
✧   My stoma will not be affected by the chemotherapy drugs and pills
✧   The chemotherapy will be 100% effective

- ❖ Our time away will be a real blessing to us both
- ❖ I will not catch any infections

May God Bless You Abundantly
Graham

"But I will restore you to health and heal your wounds," declares the LORD. - Jeremiah 30 v 17

24 May 2009 – Prayer Newsletter 44

Greetings everyone,

I am learning that my body has a reaction for three or four days after I complete a chemotherapy cycle. The effects are sickness, constipation later linked to diarrhea and I feel washed out with the added hassle that I don't sleep. If this continues, it's clearly going to impact on some future family occasions including a wedding.

Last week I purchased a cross to place on the wall in the bedroom where I can see it when I'm awake at night, and I have found it helpful to reflect on names associated with the cross, such as Grace, Jesus, Life, Love, Peace, Power, Strength, Suffering, Sweetness, to name just a few. See how many you can think of, you will be amazed and encouraged.

This reminds me of the song 'At the foot of the cross' which has such powerful words. The YouTube link is http://www.youtube.com/watch?v=Jsc1QSw6DEs&feature=related which will provide full lyrics where I have only been only to show verse 1 and chorus below.

Verse 1:
At the foot of the cross
Where grace and suffering meet
You have shown me Your love
Through the judgment You received
And You've won my heart
And You've won my heart
Now I can

Chorus:
Trade these ashes in for beauty
And wear forgiveness like a crown
Coming to kiss the feet of mercy
I lay every burden down
At the foot of the cross

© Kathryn Scott, 2003 Vertical Worship Songs   Integrity Music??

Linked to this are the words from Hebrews 12 v 2 & 3 *'Let us fix our eyes on Jesus, the author and perfecter of our faith, who for the joy set before Him endured the cross, scorning its shame, and sat down at the right hand of the throne of God. Consider Him.........'so that you will not grow weary and lose heart'.*

We had a lovely relaxing time away in Swanage celebrating Ginny's special birthday, taking the opportunity to visit Monkey World, the steam train to Corfe Castle, plus a few other local sites as well as the amazing views of God's creation and enjoying time together. The weather couldn't have been better and one morning I even had breakfast sitting outside in the sun overlooking the Swanage Bay.

Many thanks to those of you who have already responded to my fund raising efforts at an event called Relay for Life to be held on 20th-21st June 2009 at Reading Rugby Club on behalf of Cancer Research UK.

Currently I have raised
- ❖ £395.00 towards my £1000.00 target (plus the additional gift aid of £83.21)
- ❖ 4 people from work have agreed to be part of my team
- ❖ 3 people from church have agreed to be part of my team
- ❖ 4 Spring Harvest Stewards have shown an interest in coming down to support me.

If you are still thinking of sponsoring the links are http://www.donatetomyrelay.org/grahampriddy. I am surprised and very encouraged that people are mad enough to support me on the day/night and I will be in touch nearer the time to establish a walking schedule.

Further details are shown here http://www.cancerresearchuk.org/relay/venues/reading/

Next week's appointments
Tuesday
- ❖ 8.30am Blood test at hospital
- ❖ 09.50am Clinic appointment with Oncologist at Berkshire Cancer Unit
- ❖ 11:30am Chemotherapy treatment
- ❖ 15:30pm Outpatients clinic with Mr Farouk, Registrar

Thursday
- ❖ afternoon District Nurse disconnects chemotherapy pump

Current prayer requests are;
- ❖ The wound will heal without further delay and the discomfort will go
- ❖ I will be able to sleep better at nights as this is still a problem
- ❖ My next chemotherapy will go well
- ❖ Side effects can be brought under control
- ❖ The chemotherapy will be 100% effective
- ❖ I will not catch any infections
- ❖ I will be well enough to attend a family wedding on Saturday 30th May

May God Bless You Abundantly
Graham

"But I will restore you to health and heal your wounds," declares the LORD. - Jeremiah 30 v 17

26 May 2009 - Book of Encouragement

2 ....lead me to the rock that is higher than I.
3 For you have been my refuge,
    a strong tower against the foe.
4 I long to dwell in Your tent forever
    and take refuge in the shelter of Your wings.

Psalm 61 v 2-4

29 May 2009 – Prayer Newsletter 45

Greetings everyone,

I'm going to start this week's update with a reading from 1 Peter 1 v 3 – 9 which provides such reassurance during periods of difficulties, appreciating that I have had to struggle with all sorts of trials during my illness with a further complication this week. I trust you will also find encouragement in these verses too.

3 Praise be to the God and Father of our Lord Jesus Christ! In His great mercy He has given us new birth into a living hope through the resurrection of Jesus Christ from the dead, 4 and into an inheritance that can never perish, spoil or fade—kept in heaven for you, 5 who through faith are shielded by God's power until the coming of the salvation that is ready to be revealed in the last time. 6 In this you greatly rejoice, though now for a little while you may have had to suffer grief in all kinds of trials. 7 These have come so that your faith—of greater worth than gold, which perishes even though refined by fire—may be proved genuine and may result in praise, glory and honour when Jesus Christ is revealed. 8 Though you have not seen Him, you love Him; and even though you do not see Him now, you believe in Him and are filled with an inexpressible and glorious joy, 9 for you are receiving the goal of your faith, the salvation of your souls.

My visit to the Cancer Unit on Tuesday for my chemotherapy treatment turned out to be much longer than expected after I explained about some swelling in my right hand and arm. I was sent to the X-ray department for an ultrasound scan where it was discovered that I had a blood clot where my PICC line passes at my right shoulder. After a long consultation, it was decided to press on with the chemotherapy treatment, and manage the blood clot with a 28 day course of injections rather than remove the PICC line and start again at a later date. I was at the hospital from 8.15am until 5.00pm and was well tired when I got home.

In order to try and manage the reactions I suffered following the last two chemotherapy cycles I have been given an additional set of pills to see if this solves the problem. At the time of writing this it is too early to comment. Please pray that these will work as I have a family wedding to go to tomorrow at Holy Trinity Brompton in London and previously this would be one of my really bad days

Sleeping has become much better since our break in Swanage and this has continued since being at home. This is a tremendous benefit and I now no longer fear long nights.

Carrying on from the theme of the cross last week highlighting the need to lay down our burdens this week's song is one that expresses our thankfulness. The YouTube link will provide full lyrics where below is just the 1st verse and chorus. http://www.youtube.com/watch?v=AR4 . CCLnmf1Q&feature=related

Verse 1
Thank You for the cross, Lord,
Thank You for the price You paid,
Bearing all my sin and shame,
In love You came and
And gave amazing grace.

Chorus
Worthy is the Lamb,
Seated on the throne
Crown You now with many crowns,
You reign victorious
High and lifted up,
Jesus, Son of God
The Lord of heaven, crucified.
Worthy is the Lamb,
Worthy is the Lamb.

On a very personal note, my company have provided amazing support during my long illness, far beyond the terms of my contract. However, I have just been informed that the 28 weeks SSP payments they can claim will come to an end on 2nd June 2009. This is requiring me to seek alternative benefits via Jobcentre Plus, which not only complicates matters but comes at a time when I don't feel my best. I am also in discussions with my employer to see what further discretions they may be prepared to make. Please pray that I will continue to trust our amazing Father, taking comfort from words that Jesus spoke as recorded in Mathew 6 v 25 – 34.

25 "Therefore I tell you, do not worry about your life, what you will eat or drink; or about your body, what you will wear. Is not life more important than food, and the body more important than clothes? 26 Look at the birds of the air; they do not sow or reap or store away in barns, and yet your heavenly Father feeds them. Are you not much more valuable than they? 27 Who of you by worrying can add a single hour to his life? 28 "And why do you worry about clothes? See how the lilies of the field grow. They do not labour or spin. 29 Yet I tell you that not even Solomon in all his splendour was dressed like one of these. 30If that is how God clothes the grass of the field, which is here today and tomorrow is thrown into the fire, will He not much more clothe you, O you of little faith? 31 So do not worry, saying, 'What shall we eat?' or 'What shall we drink?' or 'What shall we wear?' 32 For the pagans run after all these things, and your heavenly Father knows that you need them. 33 But seek first His kingdom and His righteousness, and all these things will be given to you as well. 34 Therefore do not worry about tomorrow, for tomorrow will worry about itself. Each day has enough trouble of its own."

Many thanks to those of you who have already responded to my fund raising efforts at an event called Relay for Life to be held on 20th-21st June 2009 at Reading Rugby Club on behalf of Cancer Research UK. I am already very encouraged by this support and if everyone else who receives this update were to donate £2.00 I will hit my

£1.000.00 target. If you are still thinking of sponsoring the link is http://www.donatetomyrelay.org/grahampriddy

Currently I have raised
- ❖ £530.00 towards my £1000.00 target (plus the additional gift aid of £121.28)
- ❖ 8 people from work have agreed to be part of my team
- ❖ 3 people from church have agreed to be part of my team plus 4 others thinking about it
- ❖ 4 Spring Harvest Stewards have shown an interest in coming down to support me.

Further details are shown here http://www.cancerresearchuk.org/relay/venues/reading/

Next week's appointments

Monday
- ❖ afternoon PICC line management and injection for blood clot

Tuesday
- ❖ afternoon injection for blood clot

Wednesday
- ❖ afternoon injection for blood clot

Thursday
- ❖ afternoon injection for blood clot

Friday
- ❖ afternoon injection for blood clot

Saturday
- ❖ afternoon injection for blood clot

Sunday
- ❖ afternoon injection for blood clot

Current prayer requests are;
- ❖ My financial situation will be satisfactory and quickly resolved
- ❖ The chemotherapy will be 100% effective and side

effects can be brought under control
- ❖ The wound will heal without further delay and the discomfort will go
- ❖ I will not catch any infections
- ❖ I will be well enough to attend a family wedding on Saturday 30th May

May God Bless You Abundantly
Graham

"But I will restore you to health and heal your wounds," declares the LORD. - Jeremiah 30 v 17

5 June 2009 – Prayer Newsletter 46

Greetings everyone,

Psalm 28 v 6-7 reads, *'Praise be to the LORD, for He has heard my cry for mercy. The LORD is my strength and my shield; my heart trusts in Him, and I am helped. My heart leaps for joy and I will give thanks to Him in song.'*

Thank you so much for all the prayers concerning the wedding last Saturday which God clearly heard and answered. It was a wonderful occasion and I even managed to drive into London and back. Considering that the two previous Saturdays following chemotherapy I effectively spent all day lying around on the sofa or in bed, as I highlighted above, God hears our petitions and prayers and will answer. I did notice however that during the service I was unable to stand for all the songs and needed to pace myself to ensure I didn't overdo things.

On reflection this cycle of chemotherapy was better than the previous two; however I did have a really bad day on Monday when my digestive system seemed to start up again and worked overtime.

My Tuesday's Bible reading notes reminded me that perhaps contentment is one of the greatest things to possess – to be neither lazy, nor driven, but aware of the source of the real joy in life and that according to Paul, the contented soul is a real winner. This struck a chord as currently I am in the privileged position of having time available while I'm recovering, to focus more on God, life and much more which I must say has enriched my life during harder times.

Over the last few days a previous problem has recurred on my wound as the hypergranulation tissue has grown again. This was a real concern this morning. However, I have just spoken with the hospital, and Praise the Lord, they are going to treat it at 11.30 this morning, meaning all should be fine for our holiday tomorrow.

Tomorrow we travel to Wales with Richard for our main summer holiday which will become a real family get together as we will be collecting Daniel on Sunday morning when we visit his church in Aberystwyth. Chris and Rosie will be joining us after Sunday night following their church weekend. However I have had to make arrangements for a different medication cycle and Ginny has been learning all week to do my daily injections for a few days before Rosie - who is a nurse - joins us.

On the concerns I raised last week about endless form filling etc with my SSP ending, I have spoken with the Macmillan office at the hospital, and they are being very helpful. They provide a service to assist people in my situation with such forms.

 Relay For Life is progressing well, as currently I have raised £780.00 towards my £1000.00 target. (plus the additional Gift Aid of £191.79) and a number of people are now signing up to join us for the 24 hour event to be held on 20th-21st June 2009 at Reading Rugby Club on behalf of Cancer Research UK. Don't worry, I have no intention of being there all 24 hours, but it should be a great time

You can still sponsor me at http://www.donatetomyrelay.org/grahampriddy and help me hit my ambitious target.

Further details are shown here http://www.cancerresearchuk.org/relay/venues/reading/

Current prayer requests are;

❖ Our family holiday in Wales will be a time of real
refreshment for us all as we enjoy being together, for
safe travel and that my health limitations won't hinder
our enjoyment.

May God Bless You Abundantly
Graham

"But I will restore you to health and heal your wounds," declares
the LORD. - Jeremiah 30 v 17

5 June 2009 – Book of Encouragement

3 For You have been my refuge,
   a strong tower against the foe.

Psalm 61 v 3

Psalm 116 is good:
1 I love the Lord,
   because He listens to my prayers for help.
2 He paid attention to me,
   so I will call to Him for help as long as I live.
3 The ropes of death bound me,
   and the fear of the grave took hold of me.
   I was troubled and sad.
4 Then I called out the name of the Lord.
   I said, "Please, Lord, save me!"
5 The Lord is kind and does what is right;
   our God is merciful.
6 The Lord watches over the foolish;
   when I was helpless, He saved me.
7 I said to myself, "Relax,
   because the Lord takes care of you."
8 Lord, You saved me from death.
   You stopped my eyes from crying;

You kept me from being defeated.
9   So I will walk with the Lord
in the land of the living.

Psalm 116 v 1 – 9
The Everyday Bible : New Century Version.

(Email from Rev David Priddy – Brother)

15 June 2009 – Prayer Newsletter 47

Greetings everyone,
Nothing like attending church to bring things back into perspective which is how I felt when on Sunday morning we sang the following hymn by Thomas Chisholm (1866-1960).

Great is Your faithfulness,
O God my Father,
You have fulfilled
All Your promise to me;
You never fail,
And Your love is unchanging,
All You have been,
You for ever will be.

Chorus
Great is Your faithfulness!
Great is Your faithfulness!
Morning by morning new mercies I see;
All I have needed Your hand has provided,
Great is Your faithfulness,
Father, to me.

Summer and winter,
And springtime and harvest,
Sun, moon and stars
In their courses above,

Join with all nature
In eloquent witness
To Your great faithfulness,
Mercy and love.

Repeat Chorus

Pardon for sin,
And a peace everlasting,
Your living presence
To cheer and to guide,
Strength for today
And bright hope for tomorrow,
These are the blessings
Your love will provide.

Repeat Chorus

© Thomas Chisholm (1866-1960), 1923, Renewal 1951 Hope Publishing Co

Our holiday in Wales was a wonderful family time together, enjoying laughter, hot tub, good food... This was in spite of the fact that I had a really bad cold, which meant that on occasions I stayed at the lodge and slept as others went out exploring. One disappointment for me however was when we drove to the 'Victoria Farm' - as per the TV series last year – since, after paying, I had to return to the car to sleep while everyone else explored the farm. So the holiday was not as planned but I still enjoyed being away. Nurse Ginny Priddy did an excellent job delivering my daily injections.

The trouble with being so unwell was that I didn't feel up to daily Bible readings or even reading the books I had packed. My wound still hasn't healed since my operation eight months ago; at times I become increasingly frustrated that it's taking so long. I am really looking forward to the day when I can sit, walk, even bend without feeling pain and discomfort. However I'm comforted that God understands and this is why the words of the hymn above are so meaningful despite being written many years ago.

Relay For Life has really taken off while I've been away as currently I have exceeded my £1000.00 target. The total currently stands at £1055.00 (plus the additional Gift Aid of £265.13) and it would appear I now have a team of 25 people walking and all 24 hours of the relay covered, which is truly amazing. I sincerely trust that the weather will be good enough so that everyone enjoys the day or night when they are there - the walking, the fun, the company and other events.

You can still sponsor me at http://www.donatetomyrelay.org/grahampriddy

Further details are shown here http://www.cancerresearchuk.org/relay/venues/reading/

Next appointments

Monday
- ❖ morning District Nurse visits for Blood tests

Tuesday
- ❖ 10:00am Clinic appointment with Oncologist at Berkshire Cancer Unit
- ❖ 10:30am Chemotherapy treatment
- ❖ 11.00am Macmillan Nurse visiting me on the ward to assist with form filling

Thursday
- ❖ afternoon District Nurse disconnects chemotherapy pump

Daily injections re blood clot at 5.00pm.

Current prayer requests are;
- ❖ The wound will heal without further delay as it's taken so long but is healing.
- ❖ My fourth chemotherapy cycle on Tuesday will go well with side effects being brought further under control so being more bearable,
- ❖ The chemotherapy will be 100% effective
- ❖ I will be well enough to encourage people who are encouraging me at the Relay For Life event at the

weekend.
- ❖ I will not catch any further infections
- ❖ My financial situation will be satisfactory and quickly resolved

May God Bless You Abundantly
Graham

"But I will restore you to health and heal your wounds," declares the LORD. - Jeremiah 30 v 17

26 June 2009 – Prayer Newsletter 49

Hello everyone,

Well the highlight of the last week has to be the Relay For Life fundraising event, which was a wonderful occasion - celebrating life, remembering loved ones who had survived cancer and those who have passed away. As I said last week, I am knocked out by the love and support I have received by this fund raising event. I only did a few laps and spent most of my time cheering my team as they walked the quarter mile track from my sun-lounger. Sponsorship is still coming in… currently I have raised £1,932.95, my team approximately £2,700.00, and the event has raised in excess of £21,500.00 for cancer research.

Some photos can be viewed at this web link http://picasaweb. google.co.uk/home or in the Reading Chronicle on page 6.

Thanks for your prayers. I managed to survive until 10.30pm on the Saturday following the conclusion of the very moving Candle of Hope ceremony where bags that had been dedicated with a burning candle inside were placed around the track as people remembered those who had survived cancer, lost loved ones or those who still have cancer.

At this Candle of Hope ceremony the following song called 'For All You're Worth' by Mandy Woods, which had been specially written for the event was sung. I include it as it does make you think but clearly, as Christians, we have the eternal hope of something far more wonderful not just in the future, but as we live our daily lives.

This life is unpredictable from the moment that we're born,
We arrived without a clue to how soon we'll be gone;
Since we can't know the date that we'll be taken from this earth,
The only thing to do is live each day for all we're worth.

I don't mean to sound too preachy or wise beyond my years,
It wasn't long ago I was still wet behind the ears,
But recent knocks and setbacks, disappointments and deep hurt
Taught me to live each day I'm given for all I'm worth.

Live your hopes and live your dreams, live life for its own sake,
It can't be done half-heartedly with your feet upon the brakes;
However long it is before you leave this home on earth,
Take pride in having lived each day you've had for all
you're worth.

I may not have much money or live in a stately home,
But I've got friends and family and a place to call my own,
And I've done everything I've ever set myself to do,
Followed my heart and lived my dreams the way I felt right to do.

If I've tried and failed, that's something that I know I can accept,
But the one thing I'm afraid of is to end up with regrets;
I really do believe that we've put here upon this earth
To live each day we've granted here for all we're worth.

Live your hopes and live your dreams, live life for its own sake,
It can't be done half-heartedly with your feet upon the brakes;
However long it is before you leave this home on earth,
Take pride in having lived each day you've had for all you're worth

Then however many years pass since you left this home on earth,
You'll be recalled as having lived each day for all you're worth.

Monday I visited the Doctor as over the weekend I was suffering with a number of mouth ulcers which were becoming more painful especially when eating. He explained that, due to my white blood cells being lower than normal, I had picked up a fungal infection and the additional medications seem to be resolving this problem. I sometimes think our spare bedroom is a chemist's as I now have eleven different medications to take at various times, not to mention dressings and the two medical disposal units.

I heard this week that on 22 July I will have an important CT scan of my chest, abdomen & pelvis which will provide information about how successful or not my current treatment has been. The results will then be communicated to me in early August and, even though it is a month away, I am a little apprehensive about the outcome. However it will be an important milestone and following consultation with my Oncologist, my desire will be to return to work as quickly as possible as my employers have advised me that they are unable to make any further concessions outside of my contract. I am not surprised by this as they have been more than generous considering my first operation was 2nd April 2008. However I firmly believe that God will continue to meet all our needs despite difficulties and setbacks that come our way.

I have repeatedly stated that the power of prayer has significantly helped me during my cancer treatment and the verse that comes to mind as I asked you all to focus on a single prayer request last week is from Psalm 17 v 6, *I call on You, O God, for You will answer me; give ear to me and hear my prayer.*

I firmly believe that these prayers are being answered as the pain and discomfort has reduced in the last week. However please continue to pray for this as it does restrict my mobility in a number of ways. I'm also looking forward to organising a party once this wound is healed.

During the week I was also reading this from 2 Corinthians 1 v 3 -11 which in my situation I found encouraging with the final verse linking back to answered prayer: *3Praise be to the God and Father of our Lord Jesus Christ, the Father of compassion and the God of all comfort, 4who comforts us in all our troubles, so that we can comfort those in any trouble with the comfort we ourselves have received from God. 5For just as the sufferings of Christ flow over into our lives, so also through Christ our comfort overflows. 6If we are distressed, it is for your comfort and salvation; if we are comforted, it is for your comfort, which produces in you patient endurance of the same sufferings we suffer. 7And our hope for you is firm, because we know that just as you share in our sufferings, so also you share in our comfort.8We do not want you to be uninformed, brothers, about the hardships we suffered in the province of Asia. We were under great pressure, far beyond our ability to endure, so that we despaired even of life. 9Indeed, in our hearts we felt the sentence of death. But this happened that we might not rely on ourselves but on God, who raises the dead. 10He has delivered us from such a deadly peril, and He will deliver us. On Him we have set our hope that He will continue to deliver us, 11as you help us by your prayers. Then many will give thanks on our behalf for the gracious favour granted us in answer to the prayers of many.*

Next appointments

Monday
- ❖ morning District Nurse visits to flush PICC line

Tuesday
- ❖ 10.20am Clinic appointment with Oncologist at Berkshire Cancer Unit
- ❖ 11:30am Chemotherapy treatment

Thursday
- ❖ afternoon District Nurse disconnects chemotherapy pump

Daily injections re blood clot at 5.00pm.

Current prayer requests are;
- ❖ My wound will be totally healed without further delay.

May God Bless You Abundantly
Graham

"But I will restore you to health and heal your wounds," declares the LORD. - Jeremiah 30 v 17

3 July 2009 – Prayer Newsletter 50

Hello everyone,

This week's appointment at the hospital was 55 minutes behind schedule which wasn't helped by my needing to arrive an hour early for blood tests which my District Nurse was unable to draw from my line at home the day before. Whilst at the hospital, I contacted my Senior Surgeon to treat my wound which had again grown what is known as hypergranulation tissue. The difference in comfort is amazing once this has been treated by burning off the unwanted tissue. My Surgeon explained that this treatment may be required every three to four weeks until the wound is totally healed. By the time I had finished, I had been there for seven and a quarter hours. Now I'm on my fifth cycle of chemotherapy it would appear that the regular side effects are tingling fingers and toes - when they come into contact with something cold - and mouth ulcers which I now have medication for.

It's wonderful to know that God answers even those little prayers we sometimes wouldn't bother Him with. Let me explain: the walk from the Cancer Unit to the surgical ward to see my Surgeon is a quarter of a mile which I would find hard to do, but not impossible. The hospital runs a golf buggy service which can't get to the Cancer Unit but, on the odd occasion, does take a detour to a nearby lift. As I started walking I asked God that it would be great to meet the buggy at some point along the corridors and get a ride. Well as the lift doors opened, there was the buggy having taken that detour for another patient. Isn't God great?

This afternoon my Macmillan Nurse has arranged for me to attend their Wokingham centre for an aromatherapy session to assist my rehabilitation in view of months of limited mobility. Never having done this sort of thing before, I think I'm looking forward to this compared to those occasions when I have been formally admitted for other hospital treatments.

During July, I'm also taking some steps to try and rebuild my strength so that I can walk further which in turn should enable me to stand for longer periods as it's now been eight months since I have been able to do anything really physical. This is with an aim to assist my desire to return to work in the near future.

This week I came across this YouTube link which I first saw at Spring Harvest in 2008 just at the outset of my illness. It deals with a moving story of perseverance, quoting from Philippians 4 v 13 which says 'I CAN do all things through Him who strengthens me'. To view click on this link but be prepared to cry, I did. http://www.youtube.com/watch?v=VJMbk9dtpdY&feature=related. I include this as at times I get frustrated with the length of my illness, being keen to get back to some normality, and yet what do I have to complain about? However, as a friend wrote to me this week: 'His mercies are new every morning so although we go through trials they are after all only the valley of the shadow of death, and as we know a valley has an entrance and an exit, so we look to the Lord Jesus and follow Him as He leads us through the valley towards the next step in that exciting venture called following Him.' If you have a spare 10 minutes and want to see the whole Rich and Dick Hoyt story you can do so here http://www.youtube.com/watch?v=64A_AJjj8M4&NR=1

I was also touched by the following song sung by Robin Mark last week when I was too ill to join our cell group meeting in our house, as it provides reassurance that Jesus is my Shepherd, and as it says in Psalm 23: 'I shall not want, and I will trust in Him as Surely goodness and love will follow me all the days of my life, and I will dwell in the house of the LORD forever.'

Jesus My Shepherd
From Song of Songs 5:15

Jesus my shepherd, beloved most fair
Just the pleasure of knowing You
Fills all of my desires
Riches I'll heed not, nor man's empty praise

If you'll be my inheritance always
Your angels attend me You shelter me round
Like the Cedars of Lebanon
When I lay me down
Like rivers of mercy, Your Spirit poured free
Is the oil of anointing on me.

These are the words I will sing to You beloved and most fair

© Robin Mark, 1997 Daybreak Music Ltd

This weekend Ginny and I travel to Grantham to attend the ordination of our nephew Stephen Hearn at St Wulfram's and then a family get together for lunch at their house in Deeping St James. As I will have finished chemotherapy a few days before, we have decided to travel up on the Saturday in order to take the pressure off getting to the service on Sunday morning.

The following weekend, Ginny and I will be celebrating our 27th wedding anniversary by visiting some friends in a peaceful and slow environment that Norfolk has to offer so this will be the last update for a couple of weeks.

Next week's appointments

Monday
❖   morning District Nurse visits to flush PICC line

Appointments the week after

Monday
❖   morning District Nurse visits to flush PICC line
Tuesday
❖   10.20am Clinic appointment with Oncologist at Berkshire Cancer Unit
❖   11:30am Chemotherapy treatment
Thursday
❖   afternoon District Nurse disconnects chemotherapy pump

Daily injections re blood clot at 5.00pm.

Current prayer requests are;
- ❖ My wound will be totally healed without further delay
- ❖ I will be fit enough to enjoy the next two weekends
- ❖ The chemotherapy will be effective

May God Bless You Abundantly
Graham

"But I will restore you to health and heal your wounds," declares the LORD. - Jeremiah 30 v 17

19 July 2009 – Item for Church Magazine 'Radar'

Candles of Hope

Cancer Research

Cancer Research UK is the world's leading independent organisation dedicated to cancer research, supporting research into all aspects of cancer through the work of more than 4,250 scientists, doctors and nurses. Over the past 10 years alone, thousands of lives have been saved through earlier detection and improved treatments. But, much work remains to be done if we are to achieve our aim of beating cancer. It is estimated that cancer will touch one in three people during their lifetime in some way.

Relay For Life – Encouraging Priddy

At midday on Saturday 20th June, as the ribbon was cut, doves were released and Graham Priddy commenced the survivors' lap - set aside for those having won or still battling against cancer. Team members who had risen to the challenge of walking around a quarter mile track as a relay for the next 24 hours were then introduced and they followed the first survivors' lap as others lined the track and clapped.

The Encouraging Priddy team was made up of 26 people, evenly split between members of Woodley Baptist Church and folk from his work.

Graham receiving a certificate from Dr Christine Hill Williams, the Lord High Sheriff of Berkshire.

Entertainments were run during the daylight hours, and the atmosphere was relaxed and friendly as different teams got to know each other and share stories. At dusk, there was a very moving Candle of Hope ceremony where bags that had been dedicated with a burning candle inside were placed around the track as people remembered those who had survived cancer, lost loved ones or those who still have cancer. This bag remembers my brother in law Mike Hearn who died of cancer a number of years ago.

Graham would like to thank you for your support as he raised £1,958.59, his team topping this up to £2,700. The organisers believe that the event raised approximately £31,000 towards cancer research.

Note:- my company have since donated an additional £850.00 which brings my personal total to £2808.59

27 July 2009 – Prayer Newsletter 51

Hello everyone,

Well, how things change! Travelling home from a wonderful weekend at our nephew's ordination my wound started to experience a large amount of discharge. As it was a significant amount of discharge I decided, upon arriving at home, I should go to hospital to get it checked out. After two doctors had examined the wound saying 'mmmm that's interesting' ☺ I was admitted on 5th October at 10.45pm after arriving at A&E at 7.00pm.

The concern was that the discharge might be evidence of a fistula (a connection between my bowel and skin). So a number of tests were carried out to establish which part of the bowel was connecting with the skin – the small bowel near to the stomach or the large bowel close to my stoma. So I went through a period of scans and blood tests. Also, everything I ate or drank or additional fluids was measured and recorded as was everything leaving my body. The collection bag over my wound was extremely uncomfortable with a free bum wax every time it was changed which often brought me to tears. However I did make the nurses laugh afterwards as I explained the same hairs can't be removed twice. What became clear, as I saw a number of different doctors, is that they all agree that I have been through so much more than most; they really don't believe my body could cope with any further major operations.

The results of the CT scan didn't show anything apart from the fact that my cancer had been kept in check with the chemotherapy I had been having over the previous ten weeks. The Oncologist explained he was happy to stop chemotherapy for a period of eight to ten weeks to allow my body to rebuild itself and then to review the situation again after that. It was agreed to remove my PICC line as that may also have been a source of infection.

On Saturday 11th I went to theatre for a ten minute procedure to open up my wound to see if loads of fluid came pouring out and to look inside with a camera. During this procedure, a biopsy was taken. The results again showed nothing new, merely that the cancer had not grown and that the fluid was a steady flow rather that a massive build up.

The Oncologist has explained to me that he will see me again in four weeks time, but as CT scans don't really show anything with my type of cancer the best judge of whether it is getting worse is me, observing loss of weight or feeling rough for a few days, at which point I should pop into the Cancer Unit for blood tests. I have also been told that the wound may never heal. However, last Saturday's procedure may in fact help the healing process. So medically it's wait and see as they don't really know; spiritually God can heal - which my Senior Surgeon acknowledges. During my stay, it was agreed that the daily injections for the blood clot could now cease.

Whilst in Hotel RBH 2(as my son Chris called it) I was only able to lay on one side or the other and unable to sit. In view of this I feel that I have lost three weeks of my life, as we had to postpone our weekend away to Norfolk, I was unable to attend a family BBQ (despite the hospital saying I could go out for a couple of hours), we cancelled an open house Fish & Chip evening and we were unable to celebrate our 27th wedding anniversary.

I was finally discharged on Friday 25th, arriving home at 7.30pm, the delay being due to waiting for my drugs to arrive. One of the reasons for getting out on Friday was so that I could attend, along with other family members, Daniel's passing out parade at Sandhurst, where he had successfully completed 11 weeks of the best training the Army has to offer. Daniel now holds the rank of Second Lieutenant within the

---

2   Royal Berkshire Hospital, Reading

Territorial Army. It was an amazing day, but extremely tiring for me, so Ginny insisted that I spend the next two days relaxing and wouldn't even allow me to go to church.

Whilst in hospital I was encouraged by the following:-

Bedside communion as I was unable to get to the Sunday Morning services that the Chaplaincy Centre run.

Words given that Audrey Fuller found in a book, '*Now is the time that God is holding you in the depths of Himself. He is nourishing you so that you can rest and grow. All you have to do is to be passive, to receive and be nourished. I also have the sense that although God is our Father God, He is wanting to pour out His 'maternal love 'to you at this moment. It's tender, gentle, nourishing love. Having received this love, you in turn will grow to be more comfortable, more at ease with those parts of yourself that feel tender and vulnerable*'.

Also these Psalms from Mark & Ann Penson: Psalm 40 v 1-3 *1 I waited patiently for the LORD; He turned to me and heard my cry. 2 He lifted me out of the slimy pit, out of the mud and mire; He set my feet on a rock and gave me a firm place to stand. 3 He put a new song in my mouth, a hymn of praise to our God. Many will see and fear and put their trust in the LORD.*

Psalm 33 v 20-22 *20 We wait in hope for the LORD; He is our help and our shield. 21 In Him our hearts rejoice, for we trust in His holy name. 22 May Your unfailing love rest upon us, O LORD, even as we put our hope in You?*

The blessing of being able to follow a series of daily devotional readings on my iPod.

Finally a card from Mary Hearn which read: 'Come meet the God of encouragement. He never gives up on you, especially when life is hard, because **He has been there.** The hand that reaches out to comfort you is a pierced one.' The card also quoted 2 Chronicles 16 v 9 '*9For the eyes of the LORD range throughout the earth to strengthen those whose hearts are fully committed to Him*'.

Next week's appointments

Monday

❖ morning District Nurse visits to redress wound

Tuesday
- ❖ morning District Nurse visits to redress wound

Wednesday
- ❖ morning District Nurse visits to redress wound

Thursday
- ❖ morning District Nurse visits to redress wound

Friday
- ❖ morning District Nurse visits to redress wound

Current prayer requests are;
- ❖ My wound will stop leaking so that I can feel more comfortable again
- ❖ My wound will heal
- ❖ The doctor will allow me back to work during August.

May God Bless You Abundantly
Graham

"But I will restore you to health and heal your wounds," declares the LORD. - Jeremiah 30 v 17

27 July 2009 - Book of Encouragement

Just to say what a wonderful day we had on Saturday, and thanks to our Lord for your presence albeit in some discomfort. We do hope and pray that your pain is responding to the medication by now? As you know we pray for you every day and that our prayers were augmented yesterday as we discovered when talking to Sandra again last night. There was a coincidence at both our morning services when the ministers asked for names of persons in need of God's healing care. It appears both of our churches were praying for you at the same time. "God is just great". A verse of a hymn which we sang after our prayers was no 359 in our Methodist Hymns Old and New called 'In the Cross of Christ' (verse 2) says:-

When the woes of life o'er take me,
hopes deceive and fears annoy,

194

never shall the cross forsake me,
lo, it glows with peace and joy.

Hope this may be helpful and we are so proud of you both as you proceed and are winning your horrendous trial to enable a complete return to a life of quality under God's guiding hands.

(Email from Norman Priddy – Dad)

31 July 2009 – Prayer Newsletter 52

Hi Everyone

Not a lot to say this week other than I have done very little and taken the opportunity to rest as it says in Isaiah 40 v 31 '*Those who wait upon the Lord will renew their strength; they shall mount up like eagles, they shall run and not be weary, they shall walk and not faint*'.

This verse also links to a song called Everlasting God, Strength will rise upon the Lord. The words are below and the YouTube link is for the full lyrics can be found at this YouTube link where I have just quoted verse 1 and chorus below, http://www.youtube.com/watch?v=jP2nz6PG8KM

Strength will rise as we wait upon the lord,
We will wait upon the Lord,
We will wait upon the Lord,
Strength will rise as we wait upon the lord,
We will wait upon the Lord,
We will wait upon the Lord,
Our God – You reign forever
Our hope – our strong deliverer.

Chorus
You are the everlasting God
The everlasting God
You do not faint – You won't grow weary

You're the defender of the weak
You comfort those in need
You lift us up on wings - like eagles

Despite the week being lonely at times, it was good have the Church Leadership over on Monday night and to see my discipleship group Wednesday night when we shared an Indian & Chinese take away together, and the visit of a couple of folks, including James my boss. It was just nice seeing people and having non medical conversations. I have discussed with my boss a possible return to work package, however, I shall need the ok from my Doctor and Oncologist first to ensure I'm fit enough to cope after so long.

My pain relief now seems to be under control, especially now I'm taking the right dosage as on Tuesday night when taking my tablets, I wondered why one box was twice the size of the other box bearing in mind I was taking the same dosage, Yes you guessed it, I was taking the wrong quantity, silly me. On a practical note as the week ends, I can now walk up the stairs rather than crawl up them and I feel more comfortable, The District Nurse has now decided that my wound no longer needs her daily attention, which gives me more freedom by not having to wait around for her to call as I'm now able to dress the wound myself.

Please continue to pray for complete healing of my wound and that the discharge which has reduced will cease, as this in itself creates some of my discomfort. Oh how I long to be able to sit down as a normal person.

No appointments next week

Current prayer requests are;
- ❖ My wound will heal and stop leaking so that I can feel more comfortable again.
- ❖ The doctor will allow me back to work towards the end of August.

May God Bless You Abundantly
Graham

'"But I will restore you to health and heal your wounds," declares
the LORD' - Jeremiah 30 v 17

14 August 2009 – Prayer Newsletter 53

Hi Everyone

For those of you still looking for last week's prayer letter, sorry I
didn't send one despite a number of people asking me where it was. My
aim has been to issue updates to fall in line with changing prayer needs
or to provide updates on medical view points. As nothing had changed,
to be totally honest, I couldn't be bothered.

In fairness, I have really just been taking it easy recovering from my
last minor operation/procedure aiming to build myself up to return to
work, however certain things I have done this week would suggest I'm
not quite ready yet, but I will discus this when I see my Oncologist
next Monday. Medically my bum just feels sore, the wound is still
weeping slightly. All my tablets have warnings about making me feel
weary and if I'm not actively doing something I have a tendency to nod
off. Standing still for any length of time is again difficult which makes
standing up for hymns hard and I probably show a pained expression
by verse 2. Another issue is that my temperature fluctuates and at times
boarders/exceeds for a short period the 38° when I should go back into
hospital; however it generally reduces after an hour's rest.

I have quoted this poem below because, just recently parts of it
touches on how I have felt being fed up at home and wanting to be
well enough to return to work and have some normality back into daily
life.

When we feel empty of life and full of loss
When every day is a mountain to climb
Every minute a burden
Every second hurts
And we feel betrayed
When nothing has meaning

And everything seems hopeless
Lord bring Hope
When the weight of stolen possibilities seems heavy
When the most eloquent prayers we can find
Are tears
And the world seems meaningless
Lord have mercy

When chaos reigns and our hearts are in turmoil
When we rage against You
When our belief walks a tightrope
And faith hangs by a thread
When we feel empty of life and full of loss
Lord bring Peace

In some respects, I have also found regular quiet times difficult recently due to my tablets, however, I have taken comfort in my book of encouragement and remembering the Christian Basics.

- ❖ Jesus loves me
- ❖ Jesus died for me
- ❖ I invited Jesus into my life after confessing my sins to Him
- ❖ Jesus forgave me which I like to think of as my sins lying at the bottom of a deep lake where a sign says, no fishing ☺
- ❖ I now have a personal, living relationship with Jesus
- ❖ The Christian environment and friendships can't be beaten.

So why at times do we make it more complex?

Forthcoming appointments
Friday
- ❖ MId day Blood Test
- ❖ 3.00pm Aromatherapy massage
Monday
- ❖ 11.00am Appointment with Oncologist

Friday
   ❖   3.00pm Aromatherapy massage

Current prayer requests are;
   ❖   My wound will heal and stop leaking so that I can feel
        more comfortable again.
   ❖   My temperature will come under control
   ❖   The doctor will allow me back to work towards the
        end of August.

May God Bless You Abundantly
Graham

'"But I will restore you to health and heal your wounds", declares
the LORD'- Jeremiah 30 v 17

21 August 2009 – Prayer Newsletter 54

Hi Everyone

The key verse this week is Psalm 139 v 14 'I *Praise you Lord, for I
am astonishingly and awesomely made; Your works are truly wonderful;
my Soul knows it full well.*

The reason I quote this will become clear later but as this week
ends, it appears that nothing much has happened and yet you will note
below it has.

The Aromatherapy massage session last Friday was great and I
fell asleep towards the end. Had a great day out visiting Richard in
Portsmouth on Saturday stopping off in Winchester to pick up my
parents, however Sunday I felt rather washed out not really feeling up
to much.

My Appointment with the Oncologist on Monday resulted in me
damaging my car against a car park pillar at the hospital, this has now
been taken away for bodywork repair (I feel I need a bit of body repair
too lol). More positively it was suggested that I stop taking the strong
painkillers that I believed was making me so weary. My Oncologist also
booked me in for a blood transfusion yesterday as my red blood cells
were low, which was another cause of my weariness. I have another

appointment in 4 weeks time which is just prior to when I want to return to work as I have now been signed off until 5th October. Ginny and I are now learning to adjust to my earnings having been reduced, but we trust God's faithfulness towards us both at this stage.

Concerning returning to work, my employer wants me to attend an Occupational Health Assessment in London to ensure that I am actually well enough to start work again in a safe manner.

Tuesday & Wednesday I discovered simple things were becoming too much effort, even walking up stairs I would become out of breath and so these became nothing days and evenings I have not slept at all well, waking every hour.

Thursday I spent all day at the hospital having two units of blood and was told I would feel so much better as a result. Interestingly the additional units of blood are pumped in and the body knows how to deal with the excess blood (hence Psalm 139 v 14 quote).

Feeling better, Ginny & I had set off to Savill Gardens for an open air performance of Romeo and Juliet, however had to leave in the interval because it was just too much for me to cope with. I am increasingly aware of the sacrifices Ginny makes because of my illness and so grateful that God brought us together so many years ago and the strength she is to me, knowing that she at times also finds life difficult as a result of my cancer.

Today I do have more energy but have decided not to go mad and overdo things as the last three nights I have not slept for longer than hour periods.

Finishing on a positive note, the wound appears to be leaking less this week and my temperature is under control, so thank you for your ongoing commitment to praying for these issues and I leave you with the following scriptures as encouragement to you.

Psalm 28 v 6-7 reads, '*Praise be to the LORD, for He has heard my cry for mercy.*

1 John 5 v 14-15 reads '*This is the confidence we have in approaching God: that if we ask anything according to His will, He hears us. And if we know that He hears us whatever we ask - we know that we have what we asked of Him.*'

Forthcoming appointments
Friday
- ❖ 3.00pm Aromatherapy massage

\

Current prayer requests are;
- ❖ My wound will continue to heal and stop leaking so that I can feel more comfortable again.
- ❖ My temperature will remain under control
- ❖ Sleeping will

May God Bless You Abundantly
Graham

'"But I will restore you to health and heal your wounds", declares the LORD'- Jeremiah 30 v 17

28 August 2009 – Prayer Newsletter 55

Hi Everyone

I'm not going to say a great deal this week as in many respects it has been a real struggle with tiredness during the day and also the fact that I only seem to sleep for 45-60 minutes at a time at day or night.

Ginny and I have also had to come to terms over recent weeks that this maybe the way life will be for some months to come and going back to work next month may need to wait a while longer. It also means planning to do things is rather difficult and that I get out of breath after sometimes simple tasks. Pray for us both as we have some big decisions ahead of us and that life is rather a drag at present. Again this week we have had to cancel going out to dinner with friends.

What I would like to do, is mention Richard and Ela Salvage's daughter Stephanie who will be running the Great North Run in Newcastle on Sunday 20th September 2009 in aid of Cancer Research UK. As you will appreciate this is a charity very dear to my heart and if anyone would like to sponsor her please go to the following website: page: http://www.runningsponsorme.org/stephaniesalvage

Having said all the above, one song has repeated come to mind during this period of struggle, the YouTube version is http://www. youtube.com/watch?v=mqnbLkSgMOY&feature=related

My hope is built on nothing less
Than Jesus' blood and righteousness.
I dare not trust the sweetest frame,
But wholly trust in Jesus' Name.

Chorus
On Christ the solid Rock I stand,
All other ground is sinking sand;
All other ground is sinking sand.

When darkness seems to hide His face,
I rest on His unchanging grace.
In every high and stormy gale,
My anchor holds within the veil.

Chorus

His oath, His covenant, His blood,
Support me in the whelming flood.
When all around my soul gives way,
He then is all my Hope and Stay.

Chorus

When He shall come with trumpet sound,
Oh may I then in Him be found.
Dressed in His righteousness alone,
Faultless to stand before the throne.

Chorus
Edward Mote (1797-1874) © Public Domain

Forthcoming appointments
Tuesday
❖ Morning Blood test
Wednesday
❖ 1.30pm Doctor home visit
Thursday
❖ Afternoon District Nurse

Current prayer requests are;
❖ My wound will continue to heal and stop leaking so that I can feel more comfortable again.
❖ My temperature will remain under control
❖ Sleeping will improve

May God Bless You Abundantly
Graham

'"But I will restore you to health and heal your wounds", declares the LORD'- Jeremiah 30 v 17

04 September 2009 – Prayer Newsletter 56

Hi Everyone

This week has been much the same as the week before in many respects due to tiredness during the day and also the fact that I only seem to sleep for 45-60 minutes at a time at day or night remain a problem together with the lack of energy.

Isaiah 40 v 31, says much to encourage me just now *'but those who hope in the LORD will renew their strength. They will soar on wings like eagles; they will run and not grow weary, they will walk and not be faint'*

Having said that we have been so blessed by our cell group at Church who have moved bedroom furniture around, built some IKEA furniture and removed loads of surplus stuff to charity shops and rubbish to the tip so that we are in a position to rent out our spare double bedroom to assist or financial situation. Details are attached in case you are aware of anyone who needs a room. We have also been blessed by some friends cooking us a meal and bringing it round. To me this is GODS LOVE IN ACTION.

I had an encouraging consolation with my Doctor on Wednesday who explained I was a complicated case and that I had now been assigned as her penitence (which I believe to be positive) and she has gone away to read my extensive notes and will revisit me next Thursday,

Likewise I have had some positive chats with my boss as we work through my current situation.

Forthcoming appointments
Thursday
- ❖ 1.30pm Doctor home visit
- ❖ 3.00pm District Nurse

Current prayer requests are;
- ❖ Sleeping will improve
- ❖ My wound will continue to heal and stop leaking so that I can feel more comfortable again.
- ❖ My temperature will remain under control

May God Bless You Abundantly
Graham

'"But I will restore you to health and heal your wounds", declares the LORD'- Jeremiah 30 v 17

11 September 2009 – Prayer Newsletter 57

Hi Everyone
Not a lot to say this week but I have felt a little brighter at times. My GP visited me again this week and after reading all my notes, couldn't believe what I had been put through medically. She is not the first person to tell me this and she believes this is why I feel as I do, but wants the Oncologist appointment to take place before recommending anything else when she will visit me again the following week.

The most important event this week, is my parents 60th Wedding Anniversary in Winchester. I owe so much to them both especially as they have supported me during my illness and thank God for bringing them together all those years ago and the strength they give today. Pray that I will enjoy and cope with the day.

From Saturday, we have our lodger, a friend of someone I know from Spring Harvest and she is flying in from Belfast on Saturday evening. Please pray that this will work for all concerned especially as she starts her job on Monday.

I enclose this song which is entitled Hide me now (Still) as at times this week, I have just wanted to snuggle up n bed and listen to Christian music and reflect on life. The YouTube link is http://www.youtube.com/watch?v=FPtZRnQyzSM

Hide me now under Your wings.
Cover me within Your mighty hand.

Chorus.
When the oceans rise and thunders roar,
I will soar with You above the storm.
Father, You are King over the flood;
I will be still and know You are God.

Find rest, my soul, in Christ alone.
Know His power in quietness and trust.

Chorus.
When the oceans rise and thunders roar,
I will soar with You above the storm.
Father, You are King over the flood;
I will be still and know You are God.

Unknown

Forthcoming appointments
Monday
- ❖ 9.30am Oncologist at RBH
- ❖ 10.30am Surgeon for hype-granulation tissue treatment again

Tuesday
- ❖ 11.45am Capita doctor telephone interview to access my health

Thursday
- ❖ 2.00pm District Nurse

Friday
- ❖ 3.00pm Aromatherapy session

Current prayer requests are;
- ❖ I will enjoy and cope with my parents 60th Wedding Anniversary
- ❖ Our lodger will settle in well and we will get used to letting a room.
- ❖ Sleeping will improve (aim for 2 hour sleeps rather than 1 hour sleeps)
- ❖ My wound will continue to heal and stop leaking so that I can feel more comfortable again.

May God Bless You Abundantly
Graham

'"But I will restore you to health and heal your wounds", declares the LORD'- Jeremiah 30 v 17

2 October 2009 – Prayer Newsletter 58

Hi Everyone

Last night, after 19 days in hospital I enjoyed the comfort of my own home, the freedom to make a drink and to do other things without the need to call a nurse for assistance.

This latest stay in hospital was unexpected as following an out patient appointment when it was strongly recommend that I be admitted due to a serve infection on my wound from my operation last October. I was informed that the reason I was so weak, was that my whole body was trying to fight this infection leaving no energy for anything else. Admittedly the previous 6 weeks had seen me do very little. This hospital stay now means that since April 2008, I have now spent 16 weeks (112 days) in hospital so you could say I understand the routine of hospital life.

Currently I'm at home, having had another PICC line fitted so that the IV Community Nurse can visit me once a day for the next two weeks to administer my antibiotics which appear to be attacking the infection. I have to say I feel much better, and with some specially developed cream, my wound seems to be making progress at last and I'm able to sit a little more comfortably which is a real blessing I can tell you.

Over the last few months, Ginny and I have been reviewing my health and in consultation with my oncologist, senior surgeon, GP and Macmillan nurse, I have decided to take early retirement because of my health, bearing in mind I will require more Chemotherapy at some point. This has not been an easy decision to make as I had always planned to get back to work, God clearly has a different direction for my life now and I look forward to discovering what that is. Last Monday I wrote my letter of resignation which was far from easy, so I am now working out my 3 months notice, not that any of this will be in the office.

A dear friend shared these words with me recently, 'Now is the time that God is holding you in the depth off Himself. He is nourishing you so that you can rest and grow. All you have to do is to be passive, to receive and to be nourished. God your Father is wanting to pour out His paternal love to you. It is gentle, tender, nourishing love. Having received this love, you in turn will grow to be more comfortable and more at ease'. How relevant they are just now.

Whilst in hospital I was again reminded of Joshua 1 v 9 'Be strong and of good courage, be not afraid neither be dismayed, God is with you always'

Positive news, sleeping whist still not great has improved

Forthcoming appointments

Daily
> ❖ 2.00pm District Nurse for Antibiotics

Current prayer requests are;

- ❖ Sleeping will improve (aim for 2 hour sleeps rather than 1 hour sleeps)
- ❖ My wound will continue to heal and stop leaking so that I can feel more comfortable again.
- ❖ The antibiotics will kill this infection as I can not receive further Chemotherapy until this is sorted.

May God Bless You Abundantly
Graham

'"But I will restore you to health and heal your wounds", declares the LORD'- Jeremiah 30 v 17

12 October 2009 – Prayer Newsletter 59

Hi Everyone

This week I start with verses from 1 Thessalonians 5 v 17- 18, which set the tone of this prayer letter nicely. *'17pray continually; 18 give thanks in all circumstances, for this is God's will for you in Christ Jesus'*

Today is 12 months since I was admitted to have my cancer removed with the operation taking place on the 13th. What a year it has been and certainly not what I expected with repeated hospital visits, (16 weeks in all) and the wound still not totally healed. Yet I know, as I prayed at the outset, God has used this Cancer for his good and I know many people have been encouraged as indeed my own faith and dependence on God has grown. Despite all prayers, some not being answered as I would have wanted, God knows what is best and I have never failed to believe that 'Prayer is key not only to my healing' but life in general and even when done at the lowest or weakness point of one life, God is always listening as well as in the good times when often we forget to give Him thanks.

Things to rejoice about, I can at long last sit in our arm chair unaided, the discharge from my wound is now so small, I no longer need a dressing which is a real blessing after a year of padding up your bum so to speak, have more energy but still need to be careful. Sleeping is getting better. We also have just enjoyed a wonderful weekend away at Tony and Jackie Peacocks' in Norfolk, and for me it was great to be somewhere away from home (or hospital) since last June. I even managed to drive the 3.5 hours without being worn out at the end of it.

So all in all a good week and long overdue, but I must remember to be careful in how much I do as I'm still on antibiotics which I have now been taught to administer myself with the IV Community Nurse just visiting once a week change the dressing on my PICC line.

With al these positives an old chorus comes to mind which I'm sure you will all know;

Praise the name of Jesus,
Praise the name of Jesus,
He's my rock, He's my fortress,
He's my deliverer; in Him will I trust;
Praise the name of Jesus.

Roy Hicks © 1976 Latter Rain Music

YouTube link is, sorry it's not great but the best I could find. http://video.google.co.uk/videosearch?q=yPraise+the+name+of+Jesus&www_google_domain=www.google.co.uk&hl=en&emb=0#
Forthcoming appointments

Daily
❖ 2.00pm Antibiotics
Tuesday
❖ 11.00am Appointment with Oncologists
Wednesday
❖ 1.00pm District Nurse to check wound
Thursday
❖ IV Community Nurse re PICC dressing

Current prayer requests are;
❖ My wound will continue to heal with no discharge.
❖ The antibiotics will kill this infection as I can not

receive further Chemotherapy until this is sorted.

May God Bless You Abundantly
Graham

'"But I will restore you to health and heal your wounds", declares the LORD'- Jeremiah 30 v 17

16 October 2009 – Prayer Newsletter 60

Not a lot to say this week, my Oncologist appointment went well on Tuesday and they recommended that I remained on the antibiotics until I have seen the surgical team next Tuesday. The wound does seem to be much better with only a small amount of discharge so maybe we are almost there.

The only negative of the week was that I was extremely tired on Thursday spending most of the day asleep for some reason.

My book is nearing completion now, but I'm still trying to find a good title, my favorite so far is '**But a moment in my life** A book of encouragement in a fight against cancer' any other suggestions welcome.

Forthcoming appointments
Daily
❖ 2.00pm Antibiotics
Tuesday
❖ 10.25am Appointment with Mr Farouk (registrar)
Wednesday
❖ morning District Nurse to check wound
Thursday
❖ 2.00pm IV Community Nurse re PICC dressing

Current prayer requests are;

❖ My wound will continue to heal with no discharge.
❖ The antibiotics will kill this infection as I can not receive further Chemotherapy until this is sorted.

May God Bless You Abundantly
Graham

'"But I will restore you to health and heal your wounds", declares the LORD'- Jeremiah 30 v 17

30 October 2009 – Prayer Newsletter 61

My Oncologist appointment went well on Tuesday and they have agreed with the surgical team that my wound is healed and that Chemotherapy can begin. This is excellent news as both teams have implied that Chemotherapy is needed sooner rather that later.

I don't know how many prayers have been said about the wound but it must be many thousands by now but God does remain faithful to those who follow Him. The following song links my current feelings of the wound being healed and the Chemotherapy ahead whilst not forgetting the last 18 months. The YouTube link is sung by my favorite Christian Artist Robin Mark. http://www.youtube.com/watch?v=Uxviwvjyg1w

Faithful One, so unchanging.
Ageless One, You're my rock of peace.
Lord of all, I depend on You,
I call out to You
Again and again,
I call out to You
Again and again.

Chorus
You are my rock
In times of trouble,
You lift me up

When I fall down;
All through the storm
Your love is the anchor,
My hope is in You alone.

© Brian Doerksen, 1989 Mercy/Vineyard

I am to remain on the antibiotics until Chemotherapy starts next Tuesday 3rd November when I will be admitted to Adelaide Ward for 3 days so they can monitor how I react to a different set of drugs than I have had before. Not looking forward to this one as I have been told to expect hair loss and diarrhoea. Verse Psalm 55 v 22 states *'Cast your cares on the Lord and He will sustain you, He will never let the righteous fall'* and hopefully going forward I can take comfort in these words.

We had a lovely long weekend visiting Daniel in Aberystwth, especially as Richard came with us, spending time with together, seeing his house, his friends, his church; however I have found that physically I'm ok until lunchtime, and then when I take my antibiotics at 2.00pm I need to sleep for 2-3 hours.

Forthcoming appointments
Monday
  ❖ 2.00pm Antibiotics
Tuesday
  ❖ 10.00am Admitted to Adelaide Ward for
     Chemotherapy
Friday
  ❖ 3.00pm Aromatherapy

Current prayer requests are;
  ❖ The side effects to Chemotherapy will be minimal.
  ❖ I won't feel so tired

May God Bless You Abundantly
Graham
'"But I will restore you to health and heal your wounds", declares the LORD'- Jeremiah 30 v 17

Summary of Admission to Royal Berkshire Hospital

1st April to 9th April 2008 - Laparoscopic Operation – Formation of an "end colostomy"

A bit of the large bowel was brought out onto the surface of the skin as the new output for bowel contents, so bypassing the rectum which contains the cancer. Biopsies were taken from a large, bleeding polyp found in the rectum. The procedure was done laparoscopically which means that the surgical instruments are put through small holes (ports) in the abdomen, rather than through a large incision. A camera is used to allow a clear view.

13th October to 13th November 2008 – Abdomino-perineal (AP) resection

Removal of the sigmoid colon, rectum and anus (i.e. the last bits of the large bowel or colon) with the aim of removing the rectal cancer. An end colostomy was made in the left lower area of the abdomen, using the descending colon. This stoma is now the new output site for bowel contents.

22nd January 2009 to 31st January 2009 – Small bowel obstruction

A blockage of the small bowel which, on this occasion, was managed without surgery.

12th February 2009 to 7th March 2009 – Small bowel obstruction

This time the obstruction was managed by an operation called a laparotomy, with resection or removal of a section of the small bowel which had become stuck in the pelvis. There was evidence of recurrence of the cancer in the abdomen from this operation.

22nd April to 28th April 2009 – Hypergranulation tissue

This grew around the perineal (bottom) wound and was treated with silver nitrate sticks.

5th July to 24 July 2009 – Increased output from perineal wound

Results of the CT scan showed that the cause of this may be a fistula between the presacral area and the bowel. A fistula is a connection between two areas that is not normally there. The presacral area is the area in front of the lower backbone where the rectum and anus used to be. The diagrams below show where the sacrum is (bit of the back bone behind the colon).

14th September to 1st October 2009 – Infection of perineal wound.

On examination the perineal wound was seriously infected and I was immediately admitted to hospital for treatment with various Antibiotics and a special cream.

10 November 2009 - The Future

I decided a while ago that I needed to pick a date to conclude recording my journey in this book and this is it. What has become clear is that the cancer will remain in my body unless God performs a miracle and heals me. It is also clear that cancer may show itself in a different form hence the recent fistula. I have also been told that I myself may be the best judge as to whether the cancer is growing, the signs being weight loss or generally feeling unwell for a period, prior to CT scans picking up any further signs of growth. However I have placed all this into God's hands and I trust that He will give me the strength to carry on and face whatever the future holds.

All through my illness, I have taken comfort from a number of songs which have helped to keep me going and focused on Jesus. In this final section I will quote two.

The first one is taken from Psalm 23. This Psalm has a special place in my heart as Mike (my brother-in-law) read it to close family members in the knowledge that he was dying of bile duct cancer. I'm sure you will agree that this famous piece of scripture provides such strength, comfort and reassurance to those who love and trust our great God. The chorus reaffirms my response every time I sing or listen to it, namely that I will trust in You alone. As you have read this book, I trust that you have appreciated that even in the difficult times my trust has been placed in Jesus with whom, I'm glad to acknowledge, I have a personal and living relationship. Below is verse 1 and the chorus however the full lyrics can be found at the following YouTube link

Verse 1
The Lord's my Shepherd; I'll not want.
He makes me lie in pastures green.
He leads me by the still, still waters,
His goodness restores my soul.

Chorus
And I will trust in You alone,
And I will trust in You alone,
For Your endless mercy follows me,
Your goodness will lead me home.

Verse 2
He guides my ways in righteousness,
And He anoints my head with oil,
And my cup, it overflows with joy,
I feast on His pure delights.

Repeat Chorus

Verse 3
And though I walk the darkest path,
I will not fear the evil one,
For You are with me, and Your rod and staff
Are the comfort I need to know.

Chorus
And I will trust in You alone,
And I will trust in You alone,
For Your endless mercy follows me,
Your goodness will lead me home.

The second song, is one I sang with 4000 other men at the Mandate Conference 'Living the Adventure' in Belfast in 2007. In one way it summarises my journey which I sense will end when the cancer finally wins and I meet Jesus face to face in heaven.

A more complete version can be found at http://www.youtube. com/watch?v=P37bM87b9pg but I have shown below the words we sang which remain really special.

In the morning when I rise, x 3
Give me Jesus.

Chorus
Give me Jesus, Give me Jesus
You can have all this world,
Give me Jesus

And when I am alone, x3
Give me Jesus

Chorus

And when I come to die, x 3
Give me Jesus

As I finish my book I would love to finish on a positive note and say that I have been healed or cured but at this point I cannot say this. Despite being given a short life expectancy I really do not know how long I have left here on earth but I do know this. When it is my time to go, I know where I am going, I am going to be with Jesus. From that time onwards I will be taking no more medicine, hospital visits will be no more and I will have no more discomfort or pain. This is an assurance that only a Christian has.

If this book has touched you and you feel God is saying to you that you should become a Christian and you aren't sure how to go about giving your life to Jesus as I have done, then below is a short prayer you can say. However, read it through first so that you appreciate the whole prayer before you say it for real in the knowledge that God will hear your prayer, and answer it.

A Prayer Of Commitment

Lord Jesus, I confess that there are things in my life which are displeasing to You: actions, thoughts, habits and attitudes.

I recognise that these things serve to separate me from God.

I ask You to forgive me for these sins. (list them if you want to)

I know that when You died upon the cross You took the punishment for all my sins, so that I do not have to, and I thank You for that.

I ask You now to be my Saviour, and also my Lord.

I surrender my life to You, and ask You to live in me.

Amen.

I would now recommend you find a local church and explain that you are a new Christian and you will be amazed by the Christian love shown to you and the support that will be available to help you progress in your Christian life. Alternately look for an Alpha course which will help address some of the questions you now have in a friendly and relaxed setting. Further details can be obtained at http://uk.alpha.org/findacourse

About the Author

Graham Priddy was born into a Christian family in 1957 in Portsmouth, later moving to the Reading area in 1974, He is married to Ginny with 3 grown up boys who have all become strong in the Christian faith and are now living away from home. Many friends have been following my journey but like most people, I consider myself to be ordinary Christian, struggling at times to follow what I read in the bible and teaching from Woodley Baptist Church where until recently have been on the Leadership team. However in November 2007, for the first time in my life, I was to encounter some serious health issues, as after a number of examinations and scans, it was confirmed on 20th March 2008 that I had Bowel Cancer although I had known something was wrong months before. I gave my cancer to God to use for His good, whilst wanting to be healed, life has continue in a different direction than I had planned as you will discover in this book.

Lightning Source UK Ltd.
Milton Keynes UK
19 July 2010

157191UK00003B/187/P